Alchemical Scents

Integrating Hypnosis and Essential Oils

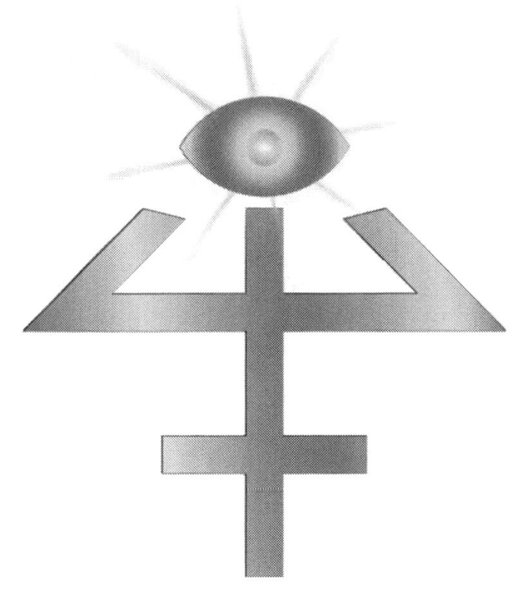

Linda Baker R.N., CCHT
Patricia Haggard, CCHT

If you are unable to obtain Alchemical Scents at your local bookseller, you may purchase it at:

www.alchemicalscents.com

Disclaimer: This book is designed to provide information on the subject matter covered. It is sold with the understanding that the author does not provide medical advice or treatment. If medical assistance is required, the services of a licensed professional should be sought. The purpose of this book is to educate and inform. The publisher, authors or any other dealer or distributor shall not be liable to the purchaser or any other person or entity with respect to any liability, loss or damage caused or alleged to be caused directly or indirectly by this book. **If you do not wish to be bound by the above, you may return this book for a full refund.**

First Edition: July 2012

ISBN-13: 978-1478141778

ISBN-10: 1478141778

All rights reserved world wide. No part of this publication may be reproduced or transmitted in any form or by any means without permission in writing from the authors, except by a reviewer who wishes to quote brief passages in connection with a review written for inclusion in print publication, or for broadcast. Violation is a crime, punishable by fine and/or imprisonment.

Cover Background Art by: Aliencat/Dreamstime

Cover Design and Cover Art by: Patrick J. Haggard

Printed in the United States of America

Alchemical Scents

CONTENTS

Foreword

The sense of smell is one of the most important elements of healing pain and illness in the body. It is especially valuable with Hypnotherapy because our olfactory sense goes deeper into the midbrain, the center of the subconscious mind, than any other sense. To achieve the deep healing that Alchemical Hypnotherapy provides, it is essential that we reach these profound depths. Utilizing therapeutic grade essential oils helps us do this.

And now, here is the definitive text for helping all healing practitioners to use the amazing power of scent as an adjunct to nearly every type of emotional healing process. It is precise, well-written and on point.

Patricia Haggard has been studying the uses of essential oils and hypnosis for several years. In this book, she clearly shows how anyone can vastly accelerate the experience of healing themselves with Alchemical Scents, and help their clients to heal as well.

Linda Baker, one of the top Alchemical Hypnotherapy trainers in the world, brings a sense of compassion and permissiveness to her work as a teacher and healer, which will make any work she does a pleasure. She has, like Patricia, been an innovator in the healing of physical conditions with light, color, sound and scent.

I once heard that the mark of a good teacher is when their students can match their results. But the mark of a great teacher is when his students' work exceeds his own grasp. In this work, I have the proof... I'm a great teacher. Now, like you, I am ready to study and practice the new frontier of healing these two have brought to us.

David Quigley, Director
Alchemy Institute of Hypnosis

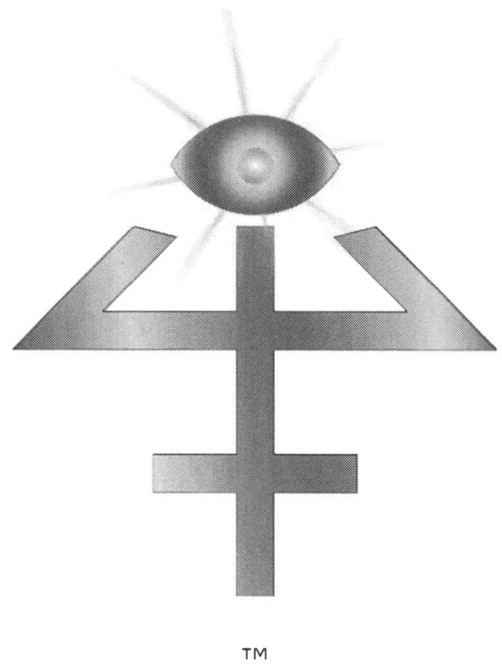

™

Alchemical Scents™

The logo for *Alchemical Scents* incorporates the ancient alchemic symbol for essential oils under the elliptical shape of an eye, with the divine spark of spirit.
It is in sacred proportion.

Introduction

This book is written for anyone who wishes to integrate essential oils into their practice of hypnosis, hypnotherapy, or trance work. Combining these ancient systems is so natural and so profound, yet still new to many people alive today. If you ever have any difficulty achieving a quiet mind (as in meditation) or a clear mind (as in hypnosis), adding essential oils to your practice may be the answer.

This work is a joint venture by the founders of *Alchemical Scents,* Linda Baker and Patricia Haggard. Much of the text is written in the first person by Linda, with editing, inspiration and a few chapters by Patricia.

Over many years we have studied widely and interacted with numerous and various systems of advanced hypnotherapy and other complementary care practices. *Young Living Essential Oils* are mentioned exclusively throughout this work primarily because they have never, ever let us down in quality or results. We write here from a foundation of our own personal and professional experiences, with knowledge of the tools we know and trust.

In this book we wish to accomplish three things:

1. Acquaint you with an abbreviated history of essential oils. This information will help to ground you in the ancient wisdom of the oils and how they have been highly valued and used throughout the world, and throughout the ages. In seeing this, it is easy to understand the value of the healing properties of the oils.

2. Share how essential oils work in general, and in specific terms how they can be applied in trance work to unlock memories, help clear trauma and elevate the spirit.

3. Acquaint you with some of the special processes that we call *Alchemical Scents*.

Enjoy.

Abbreviated History of Essential Oils

Did you know that essential oils were among mankind's first medicines? A brief history of essential oils will give you a sense of their importance throughout the ages.

From Egyptian hieroglyphics and ancient Chinese manuscripts we know that the oils have been used by physicians, alchemists and priests for body/mind healing as well as for sacred ceremonies for thousands of years, since at least 4500 B.C.E.

Essential oils are the life blood of the plant and when properly extracted, contain properties and energetic vibration to heal the body and mind as well as to elevate the spirit. The ancient Egyptians used essential oils to clear certain emotions. In Egyptian temples dedicated to the production and blending of oils, hieroglyphics carved into the walls show recipes for these ancient formulas that can still be seen today. There is a sacred room in the Temple of Isis on the island of Philae where a ritual called *cleansing the flesh and blood of evil deities* was practiced. On a trip to Egypt I was in awe of these sacred writings. It was profoundly moving to discover that my use of essential oils today is part of an ancient healing tradition.

The Greeks and Romans of antiquity traveled to Egypt to learn how to use the oils for healing and for purification. Oils were also being used for healing in India and China and following the fall of the Roman Empire, the Arab Empire emerged and drew on the knowledge gained by all of the aforementioned civilizations. There are 188 references to essential oils in the Bible. When the great library in Alexandria was burned, much of the valuable information about essential oils was lost. Later, it was only through the cosmetic and perfume industries that some of the valuable science of aromatherapy began to resurface.

Europeans began producing essential oils in the 12th century. During the time of the great plague in 15th century France, a band of captured thieves who had made a career of robbing people who were dying (or had died) of this dreaded infectious disease, were offered leniency if they would disclose their secret to remaining healthy and plague-free. It was found that they were perfumers and spice traders who rubbed themselves with the oils of several plants. (Gary Young researched what they used and created an oil blend that independent studies have proven is highly antiviral, antiseptic and 99.9 percent effective in killing airborne bacteria. It is marketed under the name *Thieves*.)

In 1910, the French perfumer and chemist Rene-Maurice Gattefosse was set aflame during a lab explosion. After extinguishing the fire he found that both his hands were badly burned and developing gas gangrene. He plunged his arm into what he thought was water, but turned out to be pure lavender oil. The pain subsided and healing began to occur. As he continued to apply lavender oil to the wounds, he found that healing continued without infection or scarring. This incident caused Dr Gattefosse to further explore the healing properties of essential oils. This was the beginning of their resurgence as healing oils into the modern world.

In 1973, Gary Young suffered a crippling injury in a logging accident. After realizing that traditional medicine did not hold the answer to his recovery, he began to study alternative medicine and was introduced to essential oils. The oils played a critical part in Gary's full recovery thus he began the journey to study the oils, grow the plants, distill them so as to protect the integrity of their healing properties, and then make them available to the public. In 1993, *Young Living Essential Oils* was established. Because of Gary Young's love and respect for the oils, his willingness to travel and learn about the healing properties of the oils from cultures all across the world, and his dedication to oversee the growing of the plants as well as the distillation of the oils, Gary provides what many consider to be the very best oils in the world.

Are All Essential Oils the Same?

First and foremost, to be of healing value the oils must be therapeutic quality. The key to creating therapeutic grade oils is to preserve as many of the fragile, aromatic chemicals in the oil as possible. In order to do this the oil must be distilled in stainless steel cooking chambers at low pressure and low temperatures. This care costs money and takes time, but it is imperative to the preservation of the healing qualities of the oil. Today many non-therapeutic oils are cut with alcohol and produced at faster rates by using high temperatures and pressure to extract the oil from the plant. Although these oils may retain some of their scent, they lack the healing qualities of therapeutic oils. Also the quality of the plant is of extreme importance; plants should be free of pesticides, herbicides and other agrichemicals in order for the oil to keep its integrity.

Some people will claim to be allergic to essential oils; however it is generally not the pure oil of the plant that causes the allergy but alcohol and chemicals used in the distillation process along with pesticides and herbicides used in growing the plant that are at the root of the problem. Many times I have used an essential oil with a client who was greatly surprised that, even though they had experienced reactions to other essential oils, they did not have any negative response to the Young Living oils I used, and found them to be very pleasant.

"I know now that not all products touted as 'aromatherapy' solutions are created equal. If ALL the essential goodness, vibration and potency of the plant are not there, the result will be unsatisfactory. (Like hearing the soup simmering all day, but never getting a spoonful to actually nourish you.) Perhaps other people have had prior experience like mine, where I'd bought some products called 'essential oils' because the theory was convincing, but within a few days after the products arrived in the nice case and with all the pretty trappings, well, I never felt drawn to actually use them. In fact it felt like a chore. A week later they were gathering dust, nice case and all. On the other hand, my experience with therapeutic grade oils is that they

do not ever get put away, my body likes them, I even enjoy seeing them sitting on the kitchen table, I feel nourished, and feel BETTER using them. Every single day." Patricia Haggard, Co-Director of the Alchemy Institute of Hypnosis.

I share a similar experience with Pat, in that my first purchase of an 'essential oil' was an $8 bottle of Lavender which I did not resonate with or like the smell of and resented spending money for. It went up on a shelf and was never used. I have never had that experience with any of the *Young Living* oils, and no matter what the cost, I have only felt excitement and joy in both smelling them and using them on myself, family, friends and clients.

See "Where to get therapeutic grade essential oils for your practice" on page 107 when researching which brand of essential oils you will use.

How Do Essential Oils Work?

To better understand how the oils work in the emotional centers of the brain and therefore to know how they can be of benefit to both you and your clients, I would like to share the following physiological and clinical information with you taken from Healing Oils of the Bible by David Stewart Ph.D.:

"One of the most powerful healing aspects of essential oils is their ability to penetrate the so-called 'Blood-Brain Barrier.' When you breathe oil molecules into the back passages of your nose, they go straight to the brain in a central part called the amygdala or diencephalon. This is the central headquarters of the limbic system, which manages your storage and filing system for all your emotional experiences....Hence, essential oils provide a powerful means to contact that non-verbal portion of our brains that stores our feelings and emotions. This is why, when you smell apple pie, for example, you may find yourself back in your grandmother's kitchen as a little child. That is why the smell of frankincense brings a Catholic back to the sanctuary where they went to church and inhaled that fragrance so many Sundays..."

And from Peoples Desk Reference for Essential Oils, 2nd & 3rd Editions, compiled by Essential Science Publishing. *"Today, we live in a society of emotional turmoil. There is more focus on emotional behavior and psychological conditions of the body now than at any time in our history. Many doctors are recognizing the possibility that a number of diseases are caused by emotional problems that link back to infancy or even to problems that occurred during conception or while in the womb. These emotional problems may have compromised the immune system or genetic structuring, causing children to become allergic to something that the mother ingested while pregnant.*

"Essential oils play an important role in assisting people in getting beyond these emotional barriers. The aldehydes and esters of certain essential oils are very calming and sedating to the central nervous system (which consists of both the sympathetic and parasympathetic systems). These substances allow us to relax instead of

letting anxiety build up in our body. Anxiety creates an acidic condition that activates the transcript enzyme that transcribes that emotion on the RNA template (RNA is the sister molecule of DNA) and stores it in the DNA. That emotion then becomes a predominant factor in our lives from that moment on.

"When feeling overwhelmed, we can diffuse the oils, put them in our bath, or wear them as cologne. The oil molecules will absorb into the bloodstream from the nasal and buccal cavities to the limbic system. They will activate the memory center for fear and trauma and sedate and relax the sympathetic/parasympathetic system. The oils help support the body in minimizing the acid that is created so that it does not create a reaction with the transcript enzyme. Because essential oils affect the amygdala and pineal gland in the brain, they can help the mind and body by releasing emotional traumas and sharpening focus.

"Essential oils provide assistance with staying centered in our goals. People have many distractions in today's fast-paced world. For example, if you are struggling to retain or remember information, breathing the essential oils of peppermint, cardamom, or rosemary stimulate the brain and memory functions for better focus and concentration. Someone who is focusing on creating a business but finds other problems that interfere with that focus, could breathe the essential oils of galbanum, frankincense, sandalwood and melissa. These oils are extremely beneficial in enabling a person to bring his or her mind into a center of focus. For emotional clearing and release, the essential oil blend Trauma Life is especially helpful."

Physical, emotional and spiritual disease happens when the vibrational frequencies of the body or mind become out of balance or dissonant with other mind and body systems. We can sometimes hear this imbalance in our own voices. When someone is in a situation of acute stress, stretched to the limit, screaming inside, their speaking voice gets shrill, thin and high. Or, when very tired or deeply saddened the voice will be flat, quiet and low. Either one of these states is indicative of unhealthy imbalance and dis-ease. It is widely believed that essential oils entering into the limbic system actually assist us to achieve homeostasis, a balance that leads to optimum health and wellbeing. For example, if one is experiencing feelings of sadness, unworthiness or anxiety, inhaling the scent of *Joy* (a blend that includes *Rose, Jasmine, Rosewood* and *Lemon*) could help raise the vibrational energy and influence the feelings of self-love, confidence and joy. If one is feeling over-wrought, acutely stressed and stretched to the limit, the essence of *Spruce* or *Cedar* can help to balance the vibrational energy bringing feelings of confidence and grounding. Dr. Carolyn L. Mein, a pioneer in health and nutrition, explains:

"Sesquiterpenes found in high levels in essential oils such as Frankincense and Sandalwood, help increase the oxygen in the limbic system of the brain which "unlocks" the DNA and allows emotional baggage to be released. Emotions have been found to be encoded within the DNA of the cells and passed on from generation to generation. Behavior patterns have even been found to be locked within families." Releasing Emotional Patterns with Essential Oils by Carolyn L. Mein

When in a state of hypnosis, receptivity is heightened. Passing a cap containing the scent of an essential oil underneath the nostrils allows the client to inhale the scent along with its vibrational frequency and may assist in deepening the trance state as well as releasing emotional patterns held in the limbic system and the cellular memory of the body.

Back in 1984 when I began to study and practice Alchemical Hypnotherapy, I felt an inner desire to incorporate aromatherapy into my sessions, but I neither knew anything about this, nor could I find oils that I resonated with. Then one day, over twenty years ago now, a student introduced me to *Young Living Essential Oils*. I immediately felt resonance with these oils and after listening to Gary Young's story (the founder of the company) I knew I had found the oils for me.

Now, after using essential oils in trance work with hypnotherapy clients and in my personal life for all these years, this love affair with both the scents and healing properties of the oils continues to expand and deepen.

My favorite oil blends to use with clients are:

Release	Helps release of anger and promotes inner harmony and balance.
Awaken	First step in making positive changes and to become aware of limitless potential
Joy	Creates a magnetic energy that brings happiness to the heart
Trauma Life	Helps release buried emotional trauma
Valor	Promotes feelings of strength, protection and courage
Inner Child	Helps connect with your authentic self

While I normally only "pass the cap" allowing the client to take in the fragrance, I have used a drop of *Awaken* on the client's third eye (center of the forehead) for spiritual awakening with good results and have rubbed a drop of *Valor* into the soles of each foot to support courage and inner strength for those clients who require that.

My favorite individual oils include the "wood" oils:

Spruce	Helps open and release emotional blocks and brings about feelings of balance.
Fir	Grounding to the mind and relaxing to the body
Cypress	Grounding and helps heal emotional trauma
Cedarwood	High in sesquiterpenes which can stimulate the limbic system of the brain
Lavender	Relaxing and balancing
Orange	Uplifting and works as an anti-depressant

In my personal life I use the oils every day. Nearly every morning since purchasing my first Young Living oil, I have chosen an oil or blend that I felt would support me best that day and, using the aforementioned technique, rubbed it into the soles of my feet. Why the soles of the feet? I learned from Gary Young that the pores on the bottom of the feet are largest pores of the body, and that whatever you rub into the soles of your feet can be found in hair analysis within only twenty minutes. I might use an emotionally uplifting oil such as *Joy*, or a spiritually activating oil such as *Frankincense, 3 Wise Men, Sacred Mountain, Highest Potential* or *Australian Blue*. I might choose a blend like *Magnify Your Purpose, Inspiration, Highest Potential, Clarity, Abundance, Valor, Gratitude* or *Envision*; or a single oil such as *Fir, Spruce* or *Cedarwood*.

Many years ago, I had a desire to bring more prosperity into my life and so considered purchasing a bottle of *Abundance*, but my goodness, it was so expensive - nearly $32 for one bottle of essential oil - I just couldn't imagine spending that much! Then I laughed as my inner guides (who have an excellent sense of humor) said very clearly, *"You want abundance, but it's too expensive?"* The Universe made its point and I did buy and use *Abundance* every day. I inhaled it, rubbed a drop on my wrists and rubbed 2 or 3 drops into the soles of my feet each morning.

Gary Young teaches us to drop the oil on the center of our palm, then bring the middle finger of the other hand down through the auric field and make 3 clockwise circular rotations in the oil to enhance the oil with energy. While doing this ritual I felt abundance in my life, and it came! My life is completely abundant and my collection of oils is one testament to that! I have taught many "Create Your Vision" classes and have given small bottles of *Abundance* out to students in those classes. I moved from a place of vibrational energy constriction to a place of openness where I felt abundant enough to give Abundance away. As I read how the oils affect our limbic system and can help us release generational patterns that we hold in our cells, I have thought: maybe this is what *Abundance* has done for me. Here is something I can do for myself every day, and it is wonderful! (See the Abundance Ritual on page 95.) Of course I have received many Alchemical Hypnotherapy sessions that have transformed my life and the use of these oils has supported and deepened the work of Alchemy for me.

To impregnate the oil with your intent:

- Choose your oil.
- Focus on what your heart desires, holding this intention as the healing action of this oil.
- Place 2 or 3 drops in the palm of one hand.
- Starting from about 12 inches above, bring the middle finger of the opposite hand down through the auric field, into the oil.
- Make three concentric clockwise circles in the oil while imagining the energy of your intention impregnating the oil – and then rub it into the sole of your foot. Repeat the process with the other foot.
- Cup your hands over your nose and take in some deep breaths to inhale the high vibrational fragrance into every cell of your body, as you continue to focus on your intention.
- It is best to seal in the oil with *Young Living Rose Ointment*, or a non-scented organic cream.

"Thought equals frequency. Essential oils absorb our thoughts. They are registered in the oils as intent. Intent is directed energy. When you apply intent-energized oils on your feet they can saturate all of your cells within 60 seconds, stimulating creative thinking and pushing negative energy out of the cells, thus increasing the frequencies of the cells throughout the body. In that uplifted state you can create a new desire to be better tomorrow. You have no limitations but those you choose to accept." - Gary Young

Alchemical Scents

When you practice Alchemical Hypnotherapy, you are immersing yourself in the world of ancient mystery schools, and as we have seen, essential oils are an integral part of this time-honored wisdom. Just imagine camel caravans transporting the sacred resin of frankincense from Oman and Yemen to the ports of Alexandria, Egypt where the resin was shipped across the world. For thousands of years *Frankincense* was transported along this path of spiritual significance, known as the 'Frankincense Trail'. The mystics, shamans and religious priests knew of and utilized *Frankincense* as well as other sacred oils, for sacred ritual and for healing. To incorporate the scent of essential oils with Alchemical work today brings an additional richness to the already potent Alchemy.

I have many scented memories, and I imagine you do as well. An old boyfriend wore English Leather and so anytime I smelled that scent I was immediately transported back in time to that first date. Growing up in New England linked the smell of fallen leaves to the joyful feeling of crisp clear Autumn days, and the smell of hot apple pie sends me right back home into my mother's kitchen. Smell powerfully connects us to memories, and whether good or bad, wanted or not, that is how it is. Take a moment to close your eyes, take in a deep breath and recall a scent or two that you like or dislike and the memory they connect you to. Now just imagine: as your client connects with his/her inner mother, the scent of *Joy* crosses through to the limbic system, linking that smell to the feeling of being loved and nurtured by that mother. Or imagine a client at the apex of sensual feeling in the embrace of an Inner Mate when the fragrant scent of *Jasmine* wafts through the air embedding itself into the memory. Now imagine giving your client a small bottle of that scent to take home to smell and reactivate that desired feeling and memory on a deep cellular level. It is also effective to take a small spray bottle, mix a few drops of oil with water, and spray the scent onto a pillow thus breathing in the vibrational, loving energy, memory and feeling of Inner Mate, Inner Mother or whatever is needed while drifting off to sleep. The possibilities of using essential oils with Alchemy are both powerful, and endless.

In Alchemical Hypnotherapy we work with archetypes, those collectively held ideas, thoughts or images that are universally present in our individual psyches. As we assist our clients in accessing the creative power of these archetypes for transformation and healing, we can utilize the scent of essential oils to help release locked patterns and emotions and create new positive and fulfilling memories.

For Alchemical Hypnotherapists, here is a list of some of the main universal archetypes, their qualities, and the **oils** that may enhance them:

Archetype	**Qualities of Archetype**	**Essential Oil**
Inner Child	Wounded: needy, depressed Adapted: wanting to please Magical: playful, alive	***Inner Child*** blend stimulates memory response and helps reconnect with the authentic self and finding emotional balance.
Inner Mother	Nurturing; Unconditional love	***Joy*** produces magnetic energy to enhance self-love and brings joy to the heart. ***Peace & Calming*** promotes a deep sense of peace, relaxing, uplifts sprits and wonderful for a peaceful night's sleep. ***Lavender*** for calm & relaxation; balances the body both physically and emotionally.
Inner Father	Protects, inspires and encourages	***Valor*** helps balance electrical energies within the body, giving courage, confidence and self-esteem; also valued as the *"chiropractor in a bottle".*

Archetype	Qualities of Archetype	Essential Oil
		Chivalry promotes bravery, valor, confidence and a feeling of well-being.
Inner Mate	Unconditional love for the adult	***Jasmine,*** nicknamed *"The Queen romantic of the Night"* possesses a beautiful, seductive fragrance that boosts confidence & helps reduce apathy, anxiety & depression. ***Lavender*** for relaxation & both physical and emotional balance and calm. ***Rose*** is high vibrational, aphrodisiac-like, intoxicating and elevating to the mind, creating balance and a sense of well-being. ***Ylang-Ylang*** influences sexual energy and brings back feelings of self-love, confidence, joy & peace.
Higher Self	Seeker; Connection with our Higher Self – guidance of life purpose.	***Frankincense,*** for deep spiritual experience. ***Douglas Fir***, and ***Cedar*** used by Native Americans to enhance spirituality. ***Egyptian Gold***, a blend of biblical oils formulated to enhance moments of devotion and reverence. ***3 Wise Men*** opens the subconscious and promotes feelings of spiritual awareness.

Alchemical Scents for Somatic Healing

Somatic Healing is a hypnotic technique that incorporates suggestion, imagery & hypnotic movement coupled with imagery of a sacred inner healer. Anyone can learn Somatic Healing, so certified practitioners are found in all walks of life and backgrounds, and many countries. (To learn more, see References and Resources, on page 109.)

For Somatic Healing Practitioners, incorporating essential oils into sessions can vastly accelerate your effectiveness. The following includes an overview the four processes of basic Somatic Healing, with recommended oils and blends:

1. **Golden Sun** process - utilizes visualization of various colors and images to eliminate headaches, the common cold, and many other ailments. (***Awaken, Transformation***)
2. **Hypnotic Movement** - a painless technique in which the muscles of the body are instructed to move themselves without conscious direction or control in order to release old traumas, restore flexibility, eliminate pain, and promote healing. Ideal for accident recovery, repetitive strain injury and joint pain. (***Valor***)
3. **Color Healing** - involves discovering the colors of a pain in the body and then easily moving that color out of the body through exit points that the body can readily identify for you. Especially effective for headaches, as well as any chronic pain. (***Envison***)
4. The **Inner Healer** - is a powerful inner guide who can give insight and advice, and will perform spiritual 'surgery' on our bodies to remove tumors, repair bones, muscles and internal organs of our bodies. The inner healer also provides daily meditations of healing which can be anchored directly through hypnotic suggestion to the pain and symptoms of an illness. The client's inner healer may advise which oils would be helpful and when to apply them. (***Frankincense, Cedar, Egyptian Gold***)

Advanced Somatic Healing protocols include **Alchemical Healing.** Hypnotists understand that the subconscious mind influences all wellbeing processes. Alchemical Healing can help the client to eliminate the subconscious processes of

disease formation, and the immune system can be mobilized to eliminate disease and restore the internal balance of the body.
- ***Galbanum*** has an earthy aroma. Galbanum supports the body systems: immune, digestive, respiratory, circulatory, and others.
- ***Lavender*** can assist the body when adapting to stress or imbalances. It has balancing properties that can also boost stamina and energy.
- ***Frankincense*** is stimulating and elevating to the mind. Useful for visualization, spiritual connection, and centering.

David Quigley, the creator of Alchemical Hypnotherapy and Somatic Healing, encourages all practitioners to use the following therapeutic grade essential oils with Somatic Healing: ***Lavender, Rose, Citrus, Cedar*** or ***Spruce***, and ***Inner Child***.

You will find some of these oils have already been discussed on previous pages; the following provides you with more emphasis on their physical healing properties. Also noted are Fragrant Influence and Application tips.

Lavender

Lavender oil is antiseptic, antitumoral, anticonvulsant, promotes tissue regeneration and speeds wound healing. It helps with convulsions, headaches, indigestion, insomnia, high blood pressure, menopausal conditions, nausea, phlebitis, tumors, acne, dermatitis, eczema, and psoriasis and stretch marks.

Fragrant influence: Calming, relaxing and balancing both physically and emotionally.

Application: Topically, as a dietary supplement and inhalation.

Rose

Rose has the highest frequency of all the oils. In antiquity, it was considered a holy flower and offered to the gods. For 15 ml (one tablespoon) of rose oil to be produced, it takes 65 pounds of rose petals. Rose oil is anti-inflammatory, prevents and reduces scarring, and balances and elevates the mind. It may also help asthma, bronchitis, herpes simplex, impotence, sexual debilities, skin disease and wrinkles. It may remove emotional blocks and limitations to success.

Fragrant influence: It is intoxicating and aphrodisiac-like. It helps bring balance and harmony, allowing one to overcome insecurities and creates a sense of well-being.

Application: used topically, as a dietary supplement and inhalation.

Citrus Oils(Lemon, Orange and Tangerine)

-Lemon

Lemon oil is anti-infectious, anti-bacterial, promotes white blood cell formation and improves immune functions. Used for anemia, asthma, herpes, warts, shingles, bleeding, malaria, parasites, rheumatism, throat infection, ureter infection and varicose veins. It is beneficial for reducing anxiety, blood pressure, digestive problems, respiratory infections and sore throats. It promotes leukocyte formation, improves memory, and promotes a sense of well-being.

Fragrant influence: It promotes clarity of thought and purpose, invigorating, enhancing and increases physical energy.

Application: for topical application, dilute with a carrier oil and avoid parts of the body that will be in contact with the sun for 12 hours; as a dietary supplement (1-3 drops in a glass of water); and inhalation.

-Orange

This oil is calming, sedative, anti-inflammatory, antitumoral, anticoagulant and improves circulation. It is good for heartburn, prolapse of the uterus and anus and diarrhea. It can be used for cardiac spasm, menopause and tumor growth. Helps with bronchitis, respiratory infections, dermatitis, mouth ulcers, muscle soreness and fluid retention.

Fragrant influence: Uplifting, works like an anti-depressant.

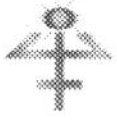

Application: for topical application, dilute with a carrier oil and avoid parts of the body that will be in contact with the sun for 12 hours; as a dietary supplement (1-3 drops in a glass of water); and inhalation.

-Tangerine

Like *Lemon*, *Tangerine* contains d-limonene, a powerful antioxidant and traditionally it has been used to support the body's natural defenses and encourage proper digestion. It may help dissolve cellulite, improve circulation and help relieve dizziness, anxiety, insomnia, liver problems, parasites, stretch marks (blended with lavender and rubbed over the area) and fluid retention.

Fragrant influence: feelings of happiness and wellness.

Application: for topical application, dilute with a carrier oil and avoid parts of the body that will be in contact with the sun for 12 hours; as a dietary supplement (1-3 drops in a glass of water); and inhalation.

Cedarwood

This oil is reported as effective against hair loss, tuberculosis, bronchitis, gonorrhea and skin disorders such as acne and psoriasis. It can reduce hardening of the artery walls and is high in sesquiterpenes which can stimulate the limbic region of the brain (the center of emotions). It may also help stimulate the pineal gland, which releases melatonin, a hormone that enhances sleep. Its calming effect helps release anger and nervous tension. It also may help with anxiety, acne, arthritis, congestion, coughs, cystitis and fluid retention. Throughout antiquity, cedarwood has been used in medicines. It was used both as a traditional medicine and as incense in Tibet. Native people of North America used cedarwood to enhance spiritual awareness and communication. It is recognized for its calming and purifying properties.

Fragrant influence: increases spiritual awareness and connection, calming.

Application: topically and for inhalation.

Spruce

Used as an immune stimulant and for respiratory health. Anti-infectious, anti-inflammatory and antiseptic. *Spruce*, regarded as a spiritual oil, is used by native peoples of North America in spiritual ceremonies. Traditionally, Spruce oil was believed to have the frequency of prosperity.

Fragrant influence: enhances feelings of spirituality

Application: dilute in carrier oil for topical application; inhalation.

Inner Child

This blend was especially created for those who have suffered from abuse. Abuse can cause disconnection from the inner child, or ones identity, resulting in confusion that may not show up until the early to mid-adult years and is often labeled as "mid-life crisis."

Fragrant influence: stimulates memories and helps with the reconnection with the inner-self (child) and identity. This is one of the first steps in finding emotional balance. Also calming, brings a feeling of inner peace.

Application: topically may be applied around the navel, temples, chest and nose.

Inner Child blend contains:
Orange - for peace and happiness, is elevating to the mind and brings joy and peace.
Tangerine - calms and helps with anxiety and nervousness.
Jasmine - helps relieve frigidity, depression and nervous exhaustion.
Ylang-Ylang - brings a sense of relaxation and balance of the male/female energies. It restores confidence and self-love.
Sandalwood - High in sesquiterpenes to stimulate the pineal gland (responsible for creating melatonin) to enhance deep sleep and the limbic region (center of emotions) of the brain.
Spruce - Helps open and release emotional blocks. Brings about a feeling of grounding and balance.
Lemongrass - May increase the flow of oxygen and uplift the spirit.

Neroli - Highly regarded by Egyptian people for calming the mind, body and spirit. It stabilizes and strengthens the emotions, promoting peace, confidence and awareness. It brings everything into focus at the moment.

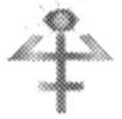

Oils for All Hypnotherapy Practitioners

Now I would like to share some of the other special essential oils for all hypnotherapy practitioners. In my practice these have been proven effective in supporting clients' emotional/spiritual health.

Single oils and blends that can create a feeling of grounding and safety:

Cyprus	Can create a feeling of security and grounding.
Vetiver	Psychologically grounding, calming and helps cope with stress and recover from emotional trauma.
Galanum	Referenced in the Old Testament; helps with spiritual grounding and to increase spiritual awareness and meditation.
Sacred Mountain	A blend created to bring about a feeling of protection, grounding, empowerment and security.

Single oils and blends that assist with enhanced spiritual connection:

Frankincense	Increases spiritual awareness and promotes meditation.
Myrrh	Promotes spiritual awareness; is uplifting.
Inspiration	This blend combines oils traditionally used by the Eastern and North American natives to increase spirituality, enhancing prayer and inner awareness.
Cedarwood	Used by Native North Americans to enhance spiritual awareness and communication. May also help stimulate the pineal gland, which releases melatonin to enhance deep sleep.
Three Wise Men	Encourages a feeling of reverence and spiritual awareness.

Single oils and Blends that assist in removing blocks, releasing negative energy and restoring balance and a sense of well-being:

Melissa	Calming and uplifting, helps balance the emotions, remove blocks and instill a positive outlook on life
Sandalwood	Helps remove negative programming from the cells.
Spearmint	May open and release emotional blocks and bring about a feeling of balance and a lasting sense of well-being.
Spruce	Helps open and release emotional blocks, bringing about a feeling of balance.
Release	This blend may help release anger and memory trauma from the cells of the liver to bring about a sense of peace and emotional well-being. Creates a feeling of being free and unburdened.
SARA	A blend that may enable one to relax into a mental state whereby one may be able to release the trauma of sexual and/or ritual abuse. *SARA* also helps unlock other traumatic experiences of emotional and physical abuse.
Trauma Life	A blend that may help release buried emotional trauma. It is calming, grounding and can uproot traumas that cause anger and a weakened immune system.
Balsam Fir	May balance moods, promote a sense of well-being and increase spirituality.
Orange	Uplifting and works as an antidepressant.

The following oil blends serve specific purposes, and are some of my favorites. I have found them to be supportive and helpful in my personal life as well as in my work with others:

Abundance — This blend was created to enhance the frequency of the energy field to support the "law of attraction", to bring about abundance on all levels of our life. When focusing on issues of abundance and inhaling this oil a memory link to the RNA template is created where the memory is blueprinted and then passed to and stored in the DNA memory bank. Then every time you smell the oil, the mental energy for abundance is created. The frequency of this oil is believed to create a harmonic, magnetic energy field around oneself.

Acceptance — This blend stimulates the mind, compelling it to open and accept new things in life, allowing one to reach a higher potential. Also helps overcome procrastination.

Awaken — Stimulates the creativity of the right brain and enhances function of the pineal and pituitary glands, bringing about harmonious feeling.

Dream Catcher — An exotic formula that may help open the mind and enhance dreams and visualization, promoting greater potential for realizing your dreams. It also protects from negative dreams that may cloud your vision.

Envision — Helps bring renewed faith in the future and maintain the emotional fortitude to achieve your goals and dreams. Stimulates creative and intuitive abilities in a positive and progressive way, moving one to take action.

Forgiveness — The electrical frequencies of this oil may help release negative memories; for moving past

	emotional barriers and achieving a higher awareness, compelling one to forgive & let go.
Into the Future	Created to help us leave the past behind and move into the future with great excitement.
Magnify Your Purpose	A blend formulated to stimulate the endocrine system and create energy flow to the brain that activates the right hemisphere of creativity, desire, motivation and focus. This helps to bring about commitment to purpose, and to magnify your desire and pure intentions until they become a reality.
White Angelica	This is a blend of 10 oils that were used in ancient times to increase the aura around the body to bring a sense of protection, strength and to create a feeling of wholeness in one's spirituality; protects from negative energies.

Using Essential Oils with Hypnosis

Essential oils are used in four basic ways; inhalation, topical application, diffusing and internal consumption. For the purpose of using essential oils with hypnosis clients, you will be mainly concerned with inhalation and diffusing, although on occasion they may be used topically, with permission.

As a hypnotherapist, you may wish to educate your client on how the inhalation of essential oils can assist in triggering memories, releasing emotional blocks and trauma, as well as to help anchor desired feelings and/or thoughts into the body and mind.

Your best formula for using the oils with hypnosis clients is to combine an awareness of which oils compliment certain situations with your inner guidance or intuition. The more you use the oils for your personal well-being, the more you will open intuitively to the oils that could benefit others.

Inhalation

There are two techniques for inhalation that I use with clients:

1. Remove the cap from the bottle and gently pass the cap in front of the client's nostrils so that the fragrance is taken in by the breath. I use the cap and not the bottle, to avoid any chance of spilling oil on the client.

2. Place a drop of the oil onto the palm of my hand, rub the hands together and pass my hand in front of the client's nostrils. By placing the oil on my hands I also can breathe in the fragrance, and benefit from the properties of the oil. I prefer this second method when using an oil for the purpose of relaxation, spiritual awareness or well-being.

During the Session

There are many ways to incorporate essential oils into your hypnotherapy session. During the **induction**, you might use oils that help with relaxation, such as *Lavender, Cedarwood or Ylang Ylang* or blends such as *Peace and Calming*. You might choose oil blends that promote courage and protection such as *Valor* or *White Angelica* or a single oil like *Cypress* or *Palo Santo*, if the client is fearful of the hypnosis process or of memories that may surface during the session.

(For hypnotherapists who do remote sessions by phone or computer connection: if your client has essential oils on hand, an application prior to induction may accelerate their induction process and your results.)

If **during the process** a client is experiencing difficulty accessing traumatic memories you might use *Spearmint* oil or the blend of *Trauma Life;* both are good for helping to remember traumatic experiences. Once the trauma has been accessed, the blends of *Release* or *SARA* (especially for sexual trauma) can be used to assist with clearing and releasing energy that has been held in the body because of the trauma. The next step might be to use oils such as *Balsam Fir* (well-being), *Juniper* (self-esteem), *Orange* (uplifting), or blends such as *Transformation* (empowers uplifting thoughts), *Awaken* (to limitless potential) or *Abundance* (attracts prosperity and magnifies joy and peace) may be used. For a client desiring a deepening of spiritual connection, single oils of *Frankincense, Douglas Fir*, and *Cedarwood*, or blends such as *Sacred Mountain* or *The 3 Wise Men* may be used. As previously discussed, fragrance is a very powerful **anchor**, thus offering an oil that was used in the transformative portion of the session will greatly assist the client in returning to the feelings of bliss, spiritual connection, empowerment or whatever was experienced. The client may wish to purchase the oil or you might include a small bottle of the oil with the price of your session.

Diffusing

Make sure that you utilize a cold air diffuser because heating the oils destroys their healing properties. Often when getting my healing room ready to receive a client, I like to tune into the client's energy and diffuse with an oil that I feel is appropriate. This could be one of the sacred oils or oil blends, an oil for relaxation, or one that creates safety and protection. I feel that the use of oils in this way enhances the healing energy of my space. After a client leaves, an oil such as *Cedarwood* may be used for spiritual cleansing of the room. After a client who is ill leaves, an oil with antibacterial and antiviral qualities such as *Lemon,* or blends like *Purification* or *Thieves,* will help clear the room.

Topical Use

Occasionally, I will offer topical use of an essential oil with a hypnotherapy client. I may ask a client for permission to rub a few drops of *Valor* on the soles of their feet prior to a session if I feel that the client is fearful and needs an extra boost of protection. I have also used *Valor* when a client's body is out of alignment. *Valor* contributes to the power of Alchemical sessions and adds to the process of realignment. Gary Young refers to Valor as "the chiropractor in a bottle."

I also may use one drop of a sacred oil such as *Frankincense* or *Cedarwood*, or a blend such as *Awaken* or *3 Wise Men,* rubbing lightly in a clockwise circular motion over the third eye (center of the forehead) to aid in spiritual awakening and connection.

Additional Facts and More Practical Tips

There are so many oils and oil blends that could be used during a session. I hope the above examples stimulate your creativity and encourage you to make use of therapeutic essential oils to unlock memories, help clear trauma and elevate the spirit. Most of the blends have names that instruct us on the nature of their use: *Forgiveness, Surrender, Gratitude, Present Time, Magnify Your Purpose, Live with Passion* and *Into the Future*, to name a few.

There are so many exciting possibilities with using the oils for healing and balancing the vibrational energies of both practitioners and clients!

It is important to understand that pure essential oils are very potent and when rubbed directly onto the skin, may cause a reaction for some individuals. If this happens, washing with water is unlikely to be helpful. All you need to do is apply some pure vegetable oil over the area where the essential oil was used, rubbing it in on top of the applied oil. This will cause a dilution of the essential oil. Another alternative would be to mix 2 or 3 drops of the essential oil with a carrier oil (such as the pure vegetable oil) in the palm of your hand before applying to the body. I have not personally experienced any reaction when using oils on the soles of the feet, or one drop of a sacred oil on the center of the forehead. A reaction is more likely when using the oil on a sensitive part of the body such as the abdomen, back or forearms. Just be aware of this and know that applying a vegetable oil would stop any burning sensation.

It is best to allow the oil to drop into your hand, rather than to touch the dropper. This prevents the oil from becoming contaminated. If you or anyone else touches the dropper, you can wipe it off with a clean cloth, if needed. Also note that many of the oils and blends are antibacterial, and so have some built in protection.

In addition to offering emotional, spiritual and physical support in your hypnotherapy practice, essential oils are excellent for home and office cleaning. The oils disinfect while adding wonderful scents and energy to your personal and work spaces as you clean. I love the *Thieves* cleaner and use it all over my home and healing room with confidence. From tough algae growth on my Buddha fountain to kitchen stains, it works like a charm and makes me happy that I no longer need bleach or other toxic chemicals!

How essential oils may be helpful in sessions

As hypnotherapists we often see people who have physical issues and while only medical professionals diagnose or treat physical conditions, we can suggest essential oils that *may be* beneficial and complementary to well being.

Valor: nicknamed the chiropractor in a bottle, *Valor* rubbed on the soles of the feet has been reported to help the body self-correct its balance and alignment, which brings pain relief. Karol K. Truman, in her book *Feelings Buried Alive Never Die*, says that upper back issues may have to do with emotional issues such as feeling unsupported or emotionally burdened, while mid-back issues may have to do with feelings of guilt, lack of self-support and self-confidence, and lower back issues can indicate such things as financial concerns, wanting to run from a relationship or back out of something. Hypnotherapists help clients to reach deep subconscious places, to uncover and heal root issues. The addition of *Valor* (either rubbed onto the soles of the feet or inhaled) can assist in facilitating the hypnotherapy process and strengthen the hypnosis session. Because *Valor* helps to build courage and overcome fear, I like to use it with clients who state they feel unsupported. It seems to bring them the courage needed to take control, gain self-empowerment and dispel negativity.

Take John, for instance. When he first came to work with me he spoke of having a domineering mother who had instilled within him a deep fear of contradicting her. He complained of pain in his upper back, where he described the muscles as being hard as rocks. Because of this, I decided to ask John if he could remove his socks so that I could rub the soles of his feet with *Valor*. During our first session, when John encountered his mother in his inner world, he froze and was unable to face her, so I reached for *Valor* and, rubbed a couple of drops onto my finger tips and passed them under John's nose. He liked the smell, probably because it resonated with his subconscious need for confidence and he was able to find the inner strength to begin a dialogue with this woman who had controlled him for so many years. As he did so, the pain in his upper back and shoulders begin to soften and release. Would these things have happened without the use of *Valor*? Probably. Would they have happened as quickly? I don't know that answer to that, but I expect not.

Awaken - This blend helps enhance the function of the pituitary and pineal glands to balance the energy centers of the body and bring about harmonious feelings. *Awaken* is a potent blending of five other Young Living essential oil blends: *Joy, Forgiveness, Present Time, Dream Catcher* and *Harmony*.

Awaken stimulates an awakening to God, or Divine Energy. I love working with clients who desire to open more to their inner world and divine energies. One day while facilitating such a session I had the thought to rub a drop of *Awaken* onto the third eye of a client during her process of connecting with an inner guide, and it worked like a charm! She experienced a deep feeling of peace and visions of her guide and of angels, something she had never experienced before. She was so excited and grateful that she decided to purchase *Awaken* for her personal use.

Joy is another blend that works extremely well with depressed clients or clients who feel hopeless. Mary came to me with a heart heavy with grief. She felt like her heart was locked in an iron box. She mourned the loss of several loved ones: her husband, her son, her mother and a dear friend. There was so much death in her life that, try as she might, Mary had developed a deep felt hatred of God. (Any hypnotherapist who has assisted in unearthing such hatred will understand how Mary felt a great sense self-loathing, as well as a deep-seated fear that God would punish her for her thoughts and feelings.) Mary had dealt with depression for years and had tried many forms of therapy and spiritual venues, but it is difficult to be happy and spiritual when deep inside you fear and despise God. During our session, I passed the cap from *Joy* underneath Mary's nostrils and instantly observed her mood begin to soften. After we finished the session, Mary said she felt it had immediately lifted her spirits like nothing she had known before. I showed her the bottle of *Joy* and explained how this blend contained the oil of *Rose*, the highest vibrational frequency oil there is and elevating to the mind and the spirit, facilitating Mary's journey to a deeply loving connection with God.

Using Essential Oils with Self-Hypnosis

Self-hypnosis is a naturally occurring state of mind which can be defined as a heightened state of focused awareness. It can be used with or without affirmations, depending on what you want to achieve and what hypnosis tools you have learned.

For many years the media, advertisers and politicians have used their understanding of the human subconscious mind to influence people. Subliminal advertising aimed at the subconscious has been outlawed, and for good reason. However, anyone can choose to learn about their subconscious mind and use that information to create powerful changes in their lives. Self-hypnosis is a simple yet powerful tool available to anyone who wishes to access their own subconscious and use hypnotic techniques in order to create change.

When used in combination with essential oils, self-hypnosis has been found to be even easier to do, and more effective. I encourage you to use it on yourself regularly and to teach your clients how to give themselves this gift every day. When people are able to hypnotize themselves quickly and easily, all kinds of other things in life will feel possible. For example, a specific scent can be suggested to bring calmness and complete recall for exam jitters, and/or to bring confidence and balance at any time.

One very excellent everyday use of self-hypnosis is for relaxing deeply. The relaxation response is a physical state that changes our response to stress. Achieving the relaxation response is proven to lower stress hormone levels and reduce blood pressure. Other profound benefits of self-hypnosis include the reduction of pain, healthy restorative sleep, increased energy, decreased fatigue, increased motivation, productivity, and improved decision-making ability.

To use an affirmations technique in self-hypnosis, first find somewhere comfortable and quiet. Take a few minutes to think about any affirmations that you might want to use, word them carefully and precisely, and inhale the essence of an appropriate essential oil. A diffuser is excellent for self-hypnosis. As previously stated on these pages, try *lavender* for relaxation, *spruce* for balance, *orange* for mood lifting, and so on. Perhaps you might spray the room or your pillow. Then begin, by closing your eyes and relaxing your muscles with imagery and/or counting down. If needed, use suggestion to relax yourself even more. When you feel very relaxed, use any affirmations that you have prepared. Enjoy the state of hypnosis for as long as you like.

If you are skilled at more advanced hypnotherapy techniques, like Conference Room Therapy or EPC, the process is the same as for affirmations. The use of the oils will enhance, accelerate and deepen your experience. For Alchemical Hypnotherapists and others who wish to readily access their own higher self and archetypal inner guides through self-hypnosis, the oils are indispensible tools. (See Quick Reference Guide for a list of correlations and suggestions.)

The Basic Kit of oils described in the last chapter of this book would be helpful for anyone who wishes to combine self-hypnosis with essential oils in a very practical and everyday way. Here are a few more suggestions:

***Rosemary* – for de-stressing when there's still work to be done**

Rosemary is associated with feelings of contentment. It's been shown to have positive affects on performance and mood. Rosemary has also demonstrated the ability to reduce cortisol levels. (Cortisol is the main stress hormone, known as the body's fight or flight hormone.)

***Lavender* – to relax, or feel more calm and relaxed during the day**

Lavender is associated with feelings contentment, improved cognitive performance and mood, and has also shown other mild sedative and calming effects. It can soothe babies and new mothers alike, and promote deep sleep in men and women. This can be a great choice for anyone trying to relax for sleep, or simply to feel more calm and relaxed during the day.

***Peppermint* – nature's 'pick me up' for increased memory and alertness**

Peppermint has been found to increase memory and alertness which can provide a great pick-me-up for too-tired, too-busy people, stressed students, and the overworked.

***Lemon* – elevates mood, great for stress relief**

Some research has shown that lemon oil may possess anti-depressant-type effects, making it a good choice for stress relief and mood enhancement. Many practitioners of various mind and body disciplines report excellent results when using *lemon* essential oil to accelerate easy access to the higher self.

For more inspiration on the application of Alchemical Scents for self hypnosis, see the Meditative Inner Journeys beginning on page 45.

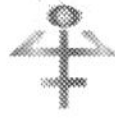

Integrating Other Disciplines and Tools

One of the most exciting benefits of practicing hypnosis therapies today is that the field is growing exponentially as practitioners from various backgrounds innovatively pioneer our work into new integrative solutions, effective protocols and techniques.

Consider the following list of inspired integrations in complementary care, readily available now in many hypnosis therapy practices:

- hypnotherapeutic massage
- hypnosis for child birth
- mindfulness hypnosis
- NLP and hypnosis
- Emotional Freedom Technique and hypnosis

You probably know of many more.

Alchemical Scents is another of those modalities that integrates exceptionally well with what you and your clients already know. For example, if you or your client practices Mudras, Mantras, Prayer, or Meditation you can integrate that knowledge into your Alchemical Scents sessions during the trance work, and/or with the post-hypnotic suggestion process. Consider the impact of triple anchoring through the channels of touch, smell and sound. Your clients' success with their hypnotic journeys can also be profoundly accelerated when you give them simple "homework" with essential oils that they can do on their own to reiterate and expand on the session. In many instances this results in empowering your clients with tools for profound self-discovery.

Here are some quick examples of how to integrate Mudras, Mantras, Prayer and Meditation:

Mudra – A symbolic hand gesture. This mudra is known to access Understanding and improves access to inner knowing and memory:

While in the trance state, the client presses the pads of the forefinger and thumb (of the same hand) together while inhaling an essential oil related to their issue. The hypnotherapist can also offer imagery and suggestions at the same time. The suggestion might be: "Any time you need to remember anything.... For an exam, for a presentation.... You will instantly and easily recall everything that you need to know, simply by connecting your forefinger and thumb in this way." (Interestingly, in palmistry the thumb represents life energy and will power, and the index finger represents the energy of Jupiter - abundance, knowledge.) For memory issues and recall, you can recommend that your client practice at home with the mudra in combination with *Peppermint*, or the blend *Brain Power.*

Mantra – A watchword or statement that is considered capable of transformation. An exceptionally good take-away project for most clients.

For example: Using the essential oil *Joy* at the heart chakra (for self esteem issues) or *Grounding* at the bottom of the feet (for grounding) the client can be encouraged to voice an appropriate mantra three times, such as: "I love who I am"; "I am safe and secure"; "I am better and better every day, in every way".

Prayer – a form of rapport with a deity or God. As widely reported on the internet today, archeological evidence indicates that prayer has been a part of human experience for at least 5,000 years. In 2002, a survey by the US *National Center for Complementary and Alternative Medicine* found that 43% of Americans pray for their own health, 24% pray for others' health, and 10% participate in a prayer group for their own health. Most people alive today will respond with strong resonance to a suggestion of prayer.

Several religious traditions include anointing the body and the use of oils to prepare the mind and soul for deep connection with the Divine. *Frankincense, Cedar* or *Rose* essential oils are very helpful. To help clients to release pain, free themselves of unwarranted guilt, etc, a trance session or guided journey/ceremony that includes anointing the client with the oil of *Joy* or *Awaken* may deeply accelerate their healing, especially when combined with a follow-up daily prayer and ritual application.

Meditation – Whereas prayer is the state of speaking to the Divine, meditation is the state of silently and calmly listening to insight and empowerment from the Divine. In the deep relaxation that occurs in meditative states, we relax our minds, or we focus upon a particular point of reference, and we take a mini-vacation from the stresses of the day.

According to the Mayo Clinic, benefits from practicing meditation include: gaining new perspective, managing stress, increased self-awareness, focusing on the present and reducing negative thoughts. What better gift to give your client, than an 'assignment' to practice a meditation routine? To help still the mind, *Sandalwood, Cedarwood* and *Grounding* are highly recommended.

Alchemical Scents Meditative Inner Journeys

These journeys are designed for use with therapeutic grade essential oils, to help anyone to relax and enjoy an uplifting and healing experience. Alchemical Scents Meditative Journeys may be used by hypnotherapists in session with a client, or by anyone who wishes to read them for a friend or loved one. They may easily be recorded and later played back for personal use, as a tool for self-hypnosis.

Each journey is presented in its entirety and each one addresses a certain topic, such as relaxation, finding inner peace and joy, or accessing inner wisdom. Because they are generic, some of the words or concepts may not fit your specific need or belief. In this case, feel free to change the words so you feel resonant with them.

As hypnotherapists, throughout these journeys we are sharing *hypnotic talk* with you. This means that we are using words which help you or your client to access deeper levels of relaxation. The tone and tempo for these scripts is very important. You will notice that we suggest using a softer voice and slower tempo during the induction and a louder voice with a faster tempo for the return to waking consciousness. As you read through the journey you will notice a prolific use of commas as well as a string of dots... after many sections. These are to remind the reader to speak slowly, with a slight pause at the commas and a little longer pause at the string of dots.

In some of the journeys you will notice that the client is asked to sense a color for a particular energy. This is because energy may be difficult to imagine, and so attaching a color gives it a stronger presence in the subconscious mind and anchors it so the client can use it more readily to return to that state later. This technique is most potent when a color of the client's choosing is used, rather than if the therapist picks the color for the client. It doesn't matter what the conscious mind might think of the color, whatever color the client chooses during this altered state is the right one.

You will also notice that during some of the journeys the client is asked ahead of time to select a finger that can be raised when a certain question is asked. This allows the sub-conscious mind to communicate with the facilitator directly so that the client's trance state is not interrupted. In hypnosis this is called an ideomotor signal.

These journeys are meant to enhance relaxation and personal growth and to complement well-being. They are in no way intended to replace medical treatment. If anyone has feelings or thoughts of harm, or is unable to perform daily tasks, seek medical attention.

It is unlikely, but should you become anxious, sad or angry while using these journeys, it may be because a subconscious memory has been activated. In that case, you may wish to consider professional hypnotherapy sessions with an Alchemical Hypnotherapist.

We hope that you and your clients benefit from these sessions and we welcome your comments and feedback.

See page 108 for contact information.

Journey to the Temple of Wisdom

The intention of this guided, inner journey, is for the recipient to travel to a sacred temple to meet with Spirit Guides, Divine/God Source Energy and or Etheric Beings that can offer wisdom, cleansing and healing (on the physical, emotional, mental levels ... whatever is needed by the recipient.)

My favorite essential oil for this journey is *Awaken*, a special Young Living blend designed to help bring one to inner knowledge. I have experienced success with this journey in my own life and with clients wishing to make changes and transitions, and generally helping people to reach their highest potential. If the blend *Awaken* is not available, you can substitute *Frankincense.* Known and highly regarded as *The Holy Anointing Oil of the Middle East,* Frankincense is high in sesquiterpenes and elevating to the mind. The blends *Inspiration* and *3 Wise Men* contain *Frankincense* thus are also good alternatives to *Awaken*.

A drop of *Awaken* rubbed clockwise over the Ajna Chakra (the sixth primary chakra according to Hindu tradition) penetrates the skin and may awaken the third eye. The high levels of sesquiterpenes found in essential oils, and especially in some of the oils of this blend, help increase the flow of oxygen to the limbic system of the brain, unlocking DNA and facilitating release of old, negative emotions. The third eye, located at the Ajna Chakra (above the nose and between the eyebrows) is the gate to higher consciousness, visions, intuition, clairvoyance and eventual enlightenment. The potent fragrant influence of *Awaken* supports creativity of the right brain and enhances the function of the pineal and pituitary glands to balance the energy centers of the body. Because scent travels straight from the olfactory nerves to the hippocampus (the memory and emotion center of the brain) aroma is valuable in assisting with the unlocking of memories. See pages 9 to 11 of this book.

The following journey script is written for the therapist to present to a client, but may easily be read and recorded and later played back for personal use. It is designed to work with the client's own belief system, to help the client connect to their source energy, however they define that.

Preparing for the Journey:

Before the journey begins ask the client to describe their spiritual belief, or faith system. Who or what does your client connect to on a spiritual level? It doesn't matter who or what this is, but it is important for you to know, as you will need this information for the induction and journey portions of this exercise. Spiritual connections can include, but are not limited to: God, Power Animals, Spirit Guides, Source Energy, Angels, Buddha, Jesus, Mohammed or Nature Beings. It is important that the client chooses what will be used as this will increase the safety and potency of the exercise.

Also, inform the client that during the journey they will have an opportunity to make a sacred connection, and that you will wait quietly while the client has this experience. Tell the client that when their sacred connection is complete, they will signal you by raising the index finger on one hand, to let you know that it is time to move on. Have the client establish this by raising that finger right now, so that later you will know which finger it will be.

There are 3 parts to this journey:
The induction
The journey
The return to full awakened consciousness

Provide a comfortable, safe place where the client can sit or lie down in total relaxation. In preparing for this journey, make certain all electronic devices are turned off and that any potential distractions are removed. To ensure your client receives full benefit from this experience, plan approximately 45 to 60 minutes of undisturbed time. For a first time experience, there may be some normal hesitation or fear in letting go; a client who is already comfortable with the trance state may go much deeper. You may wish to make it

clear that **the client** will control the pace during this safe process, and can go as deeply as they feel comfortable with.

When the client is in position, ask if you may rub one drop of Awaken (or substitute oil) on the Ajna Chakra. With their permission, you then place a drop on your finger and gently rub it onto the forehead, spreading the oil in clockwise circles with the intention of opening the third eye. Then, pass your fingers under the client's nostrils to engage the olfactory sense.

Journey to the Temple of Wisdom:

Use a slow tempo with a soft, soothing voice throughout this induction. Instruct the client to close their eyes (if they have not already done so) and to take some nice deep breaths. The voice of the therapist is bold font and italicized:

As you feel the breath enter and release from the body, you feel yourself sinking deeper into a place of peace and relaxation. During this time, you focus and observe the client's rising and falling chest, using the word ***"enter"*** as the client breathes in and ***"release"*** as the client exhales. This creates rapport, which helps the client to relax and go deeper.

After 3 – 5 deep breaths continue:

And now you might even begin to feel warm and gentle waves of relaxation beginning at the soles of your feet, to gently and slowly rise up through your ankles, up through the calves of your legs and into the knee joints. Each wave of relaxation helps you to let go and sink even deeper within... as these warm and gentle waves of relaxation rise into the muscles of the thighs and up through the groin, pelvis and buttocks, you allow yourself to relax even more. You might even feel a sense of peace as you let go and allow these waves of relaxation to rise into the abdomen, relaxing all the organs here and gently move into the lower back relaxing all the muscles there .... the waves of relaxation continue to move into the mid back, and into the upper back, relaxing, warming and soothing the muscles

as they even fill the chest with warm relaxation, allowing the heart to beat so easily and the lungs to breathe so effortlessly .... the waves of relaxation flow upwards through the neck and into the muscles of the jaw. You might even notice the jaw just drop ever so slightly as it fills with these comforting waves of relaxation ....as these warm waves fill the muscles of the cheeks and the muscles around the eyes with gentle relaxation you can even allow yourself to sink even deeper, and deeper as you may notice the eyelids becoming so heavy, so relaxed as these gentle waves rise up to the top of the head and even down into the brain itself, allowing the brain to relax and let go......

And here in this place you can even imagine a stairway of ten steps, a stairway of whatever kind you imagine, one that takes you up to that Temple of Wisdom. The temple where you can connect with _______ (what/who the client told you prior to the session – for this example I will use spirit guides) ***your spirit guides and to find the wisdom that you are seeking.***

So, stepping on step number 10, feeling the step beneath your foot as you allow yourself to sink even deeper...

and 9, knowing that only that which is for your highest and greatest good can enter into this place ...

and 8, with each count you allow yourself to sink even deeper within ...

and 7, each step carrying you even deeper into that place of peace and inner wisdom...

and 6, calling here upon your spirit guides, those who love you so dearly, who know your heart's desire to be here with you NOW, to guide you on this journey ...

and as you sink even deeper, 5

and 4, feeling your own willingness to know what you may need to know, to release all energy that does not serve your highest good and to receive the gifts your guides have for you today ...

and 3, allowing all the cells of your body to open to inner knowing

and 2,

and 1, coming to the top of that stairway and finding yourself in a very special place, who knows, maybe a place like you have never experienced before. Take a moment to breathe in the energy of this place (a good time to begin to pass the cap from *Awaken* underneath the client's nose so that they may smell the fragrance. Continue this as often as you feel drawn to throughout the journey) ***and notice how it feels to be here. You might even sense that there is a pathway for you to follow, a pathway that leads to the Temple of Wisdom. As you begin to walk down this path you might sense what is around you, maybe through noticing the sights, or hearing the sounds or by having an inner feeling of how it is to be here.... as you follow this path you might even be aware that it turns a corner and that you feel a bit of anticipation or even excitement as you know that the Temple of Wisdom is waiting around that corner for you. That's right, in just a moment you turn that corner and find the Temple of Wisdom. You might see or sense it in some way. You can feel the energy of it and maybe that energy even becomes stronger with each step that you take toward it. You may even sense that the temple is open and as you come closer you might sense, or notice beings at the opening, beings who are there to greet you and welcome you into the temple. You may recognize them as your own spirit guides*** (or whomever the client told you about before the journey began), or they may be new to you.

Take a moment to breathe and feel their energy... and allow them to guide you inside to a very special place, a place where you can easily go to experience what you need here. Allowing yourself to settle into this comfortable

place and in just a moment these beings will answer your questions and maybe even show you some special things that are for your highest good. You can ask them whatever you like and easily sense or hear the answers. I will be waiting. You can easily raise the index finger of your *(the hand designated by the client; left or right)* ______ ***hand when you are ready to go on. Allow yourself to sink into that place of Divine Wisdom, NOW.***

Quietly wait for the client to move their finger. If sufficient time has passed and there is no finger movement you may suggest that ***"...Maybe now or in a moment you will know that it is time to move on and that finger will signal to me"***

After the signal:
And now it is time to leave this place. You may wish to ask your guides if there is anything more that they want to share with you, or if there is a gift they have for you. Wait for a moment, and then go on: ***If there is a gift, you can sense and know its purpose. You can take this gift and all the wisdom that you have gained and place it in your body, maybe in or near to your heart or any place which is right for you. You know that you can access this at any time just by remembering it here within you, or by gently touching this place on your body. A touch activates the gift, it activates the wisdom. And every time you breathe in the fragrance of Awaken*** (or other oil used), ***you are immediately transported to this inner Temple of Wisdom, you immediately feel that sense of peace and you receive inner wisdom. It's so good to know that you have all these ways of returning to this place, at any time you desire to. This Temple of Wisdom is always here for you.***

Now, it's time to say goodbye to this place. It's so good to know that you can return here anytime you wish to experience this peaceful feeling, to meet with these special beings and to learn more wisdom. But now it is time to say goodbye and to thank them for all that they have shared with you. Now it's time to imagine a stairway of 5 steps, 5 steps that can take you back to the present time _______ (insert today's day and date here).

Speaking in an energetic voice –

Counting back now,

and:

1; remembering everything you wish to remember from this time, clearly and easily

2; returning back into this present time of ________, feeling refreshed, relaxed and ready to use this wisdom in your present day life

3; feeling so very good about yourself, so good about who you are

4; beginning to stretch and move your arms and legs, to open and close your fingers

and

5; opening yours eyes and being fully present, fully awake and fully aware, remembering all that you wish to remember.

Give the client a few moments to become fully awake and aware. Make sure that water is available and suggest that the client may feel like sharing part of this inner journey with you; or the client might prefer to keep quiet and process it later, at their own pace.

As a powerful tool for returning to this inner place and for remembering the information learned, the client may wish to obtain the essential oil used during the journey. If you have a supply on hand, you could give them a small sample to take away and practice with on their own. Remember to remind the client that this inner place can be accessed by them without the use of the oil.

Opening the Door to Joy

From a combination of seeing clients and listening to the news, I have learned that energy in the exterior world contributes a great deal to personal chaos and depression, hopelessness, lack of passion and low motivation on the inside. It seems that more than ever we are in need of clearing out the old energies of our personal past so that we can live in our center of joy, the way we were meant to live.

Holding on to past traumas and beliefs has become a way of life for many people; although there may be a deep inner longing to be set free and live in the lightness of joy, there doesn't seem to be a way out or a way to let go. I often find people who unconsciously identify with the heavy energies of depression, discouragement, disappointment and hopelessness and are unable to completely shake off the gray cloud that seems attached to their aura and steals away their sense of well-being.

Can using essential oils guarantee that the clouds will lift? No, of course not; nothing delivers that guarantee. What I can say is that in my experience, using specific oils in combination with the following meditative guided journey can offer relief and open the heart and mind to the sunshine of life. It is helpful on a daily basis initially, tapering off to once a week, or on an as-needed basis.

This meditation may be helpful to anyone who experiences occasional depression, hopelessness, discouragement and disappointment, lack of passion or motivation in life. Remember: this is not meant to take the place of medical treatment and if anyone has any thoughts of suicide, of harming themselves or another, or is unable to perform responsibilities at work or at home, advice of a medical professional should be obtained.

There are several oils that may be used in conjunction with this meditative inner journey. *Joy* is one of my favorites, as it has worked especially well with clients challenged by occasional depression. *Joy* does exactly what it says ... it brings the essence of joy into one's life. Other blends that may be used are:

Valor, if courage is lacking
Sacred Mountain, if the issue is concerned with finding inner peace
Passion, if there is a lack of passion or motivation in life
Hope, if a feeling of hopelessness is the issue
Present Time if the challenge is living in the past or the future
Envision if faith in the future and in achieving one's goals and dreams is needed
Release and *Acceptance* are also supportive and may be used during this process where noted.

The intention of this journey is to release that which stands in the way of inner joy, passion, motivation and love of life and self, and flood the cells with new energy that allows the physical, mental, emotional and spiritual bodies to accept this new energy. *Release* helps release anger and memory trauma from the cells of the liver as well as letting go of negative emotions so that feelings of harmony and balance within the mind and body are stimulated. *Acceptance* stimulates the mind, compelling it to open and accept new things in life.

Preparing for the Journey:

The following meditative journey script is written for the therapist to present to a client, but may easily be read and recorded so that it may be played back for personal use.

There are 3 parts to this journey:

- The induction
- The journey – stepping behind a door to release what needs to be released, to have the joy that you desire
- The return to full awakened consciousness

Provide a comfortable, safe place where the client can sit or lie down in total relaxation. In preparing for this journey, make certain all electronic devices are turned off and that any potential distractions are removed. To ensure your client

receives full benefit from this experience, plan approximately 45 to 60 minutes of undisturbed time. For a first time experience, there may be some normal hesitation or fear in letting go; a client who is already comfortable with the trance state may go much deeper. You may wish to make it clear that **the client** will control the pace during this safe process, and can go as deeply as they feel comfortable with.

Before the journey begins ask if it is OK to use the words *"Spirit Guides"* and *"Helpers"*. The intent is to honor and respect that we are working with Divine Energy, as the energy that heals. If these words are not OK with the client, take note of what words they would rather have you use.

Also, inform the client that during the journey they will have an opportunity to clear out old energy, and that you will wait quietly while they complete this process. Tell the client that when their clearing process is complete, they will signal you by raising the index finger on one hand, to let you know that it is time to move on. Have the client establish this by raising that finger right now, so that later you will know which finger it will be.

When the client is in position, lying or sitting comfortably, invite the client to receive one-to-three drops of *Joy* onto the fingers of their right hand, which they can gently rub onto the area of the physical heart while, at the same time, setting the intention of bringing joy to this heart. If the client's need is for courage, you might also ask for permission to rub a few drops of *Valor* onto the soles of the feet. (I have experienced good results in doing this with clients as it does seem to enhance their ability to find inner strength.) For the other blends, during the journey you can pass the cap of the bottle underneath the client's nostrils to engage the olfactory senses and carry the fragrance of the oils into their journey.

Opening the Door to Joy:

Use a slow tempo with a soft, soothing voice throughout this induction. Instruct the client to close their eyes (if they have not

already done so) and to take some nice deep breaths. The voice of the therapist is in bold font and italicized:

As you feel the breath enter and release from the body, you feel yourself sinking deeply into a place of peace and relaxation. During this time, you focus and observe the client's rising and falling chest, using the word ***"enter"*** as the client breathes in and ***"release"*** as the client exhales. This creates rapport, which helps the client to relax and go deeper.

After 3 – 5 deep breaths continue:

And now you might even begin to feel warm and gentle waves of relaxation beginning at the soles of your feet, to gently and slowly rise up through your ankles, up through the calves of your legs and into the knee joints. Each wave of relaxation helps you to let go and sink even deeper within... as these warm and gentle waves of relaxation rise into the muscles of the thighs and up through the groin, pelvis and buttocks, you allow yourself to relax even more. You might even feel a sense of peace as you let go and allow these waves of relaxation to rise into the abdomen, relaxing all the organs here and gently move into the lower back relaxing all the muscles there .... the waves of relaxation continue to move into the mid back, and into the upper back, relaxing, warming and soothing the muscles as they even fill the chest with warm relaxation, allowing the heart to beat so easily and the lungs to breathe so effortlessly .... the waves of relaxation flow upwards through the neck and into the muscles of the jaw. You might even notice the jaw just drop ever so slightly as it fills with these comforting waves of relaxation ....as these warm waves fill the muscles of the cheeks and the muscles around the eyes with gentle relaxation you can even allow yourself to sink even deeper, and deeper as you may notice the eyelids becoming so heavy, so relaxed as these gentle waves rise up to the top of the head and even down into the brain itself, allowing the brain to relax and let go......

And here in this place you can even imagine a stairway of ten steps, a stairway of whatever kind you imagine, one that takes you down, down to a special doorway, and behind that door you can easily enter into the inner place where that identification with _________ (depression, hopelessness, lack of motivation, lack of passion or whatever it is that the client may be feeling) ***is held. Your mind may not know where this is held, but your body does and your body can take you there. And here you can release this old energy and bring in that feeling of*** _________ (joy, passion, motivation, happiness, inner peace – whatever it is that the client is looking for) ***so easily, so effortlessly. And now stepping onto step number 10, feeling the step beneath your foot as you allow yourself to sink even deeper...***

and 9, knowing only that which is for your highest and greatest good can enter into this place ...

and 8, with each count you allow yourself to sink even deeper within ...

and 7, each step carrying you even deeper into that place of peace and inner wisdom...

and 6, calling here upon your spirit guides, those who love you so dearly, who know your heart's desire, to be here with you NOW, to guide you on this journey ...

as you sink even deeper ...

and 5 ...

and 4, feeling your own willingness to know what you may need to know, to release all energy that does not serve your highest good and to receive the gifts your guides have for you today ...

and 3, allowing all the cells of your body to open to memory and inner knowing

and 2 ... closer to that door or opening

and 1 ...

Finding yourself at a door ... and maybe now ... or in a moment ... you can open that door and step to the other side, into that place or room that holds the old memories, beliefs and feelings that keep you from feeling and living (having) ***the*** _______ (joy, passion, motivation, peace) ***that you desire. Just take a moment to sense what these things might be. Maybe it's something someone told you, or something that happened to you in the past .. just be still and be aware ...***

(Give the client one or two minutes to become in touch with these things – remember that a very short time in waking consciousness can feel like a long time in trance). At this time, you may pass the cap of the bottle of *Release* in front of the client's nostrils, slowly, several times so that they take in the vibrational fragrance which assists in the process of release.

Continuing:

Now you can easily imagine a window in this room, and outside the window is a big garbage truck, because all that is in this room is just old garbage, old junk that you have collected, and it has no place in your new life. So, in your own way, with the help of your spirit guides and helpers, you can begin to throw all that old garbage out of the window and into the truck. Take your time. Make sure to get it all out, and when you have finished, raise that finger and let me know.

Watch for the raised finger, then continue: ***Yes, that's right, it's all in that truck now, and now that truck is driving away ... driving further and further away ... driving out of sight, never to return, never to come back*** (with this you are creating a sense that this old garbage is permanently removed from the client's life).

And now asking your spirit guides and helpers to use their magic to completely and fully cleanse this space ... maybe

they wash it down, or use fairy dust or anything else that you wish them to do. ... Now take in a long, deep breath and sense how it feels to be here in this clean space. (At this time, if you have *Acceptance*, pass the cap several times underneath the nostrils so the client can benefit from a feeling of confidence and striving toward a higher potential which are the fragrant influences of *Acceptance*.)

And now breathe in and feel that feeling of _____ (joy, hope, inner peace, passion, motivation ... whatever it was that the client was asking for.) This is the perfect time to take that bottle of *Joy, Sacred Mountain, Acceptance, Passion, Hope, Envision, Present Time* or other oil of your choice and pass the cap underneath the client's nostrils, while instructing them to breathe the fragrant influence deeply into their body. For example, with using *Joy*, I would say:

And now you can breathe deeply, taking in the fragrance of Joy and letting it fill this space with self-love, confidence and happiness. Breathe it into every cell of your body and sense if there is a color that symbolizes this fragrance. If there is, breathe this color into this space, filling it with this color and filling every cell of your body with this color.

Alternatively, ask the client to tell you if there is a color that they associate with the oil. This is preferable, as it is more powerful for them to use their own color. This would be done in this way:

And now you can breathe deeply, taking in the fragrance of Joy and letting it fill this space with self-love, confidence and happiness. Breathe it into every cell of your body and sense if there is a color that symbolizes this fragrance, and if there is, you can easily speak aloud and tell me what that color is. That's right; it's pink *(or whatever color the client expressed),* ***and now you can breathe pink into that space and into every cell of your body. Feel how it feels to breathe in the scent of Joy and to fill your body with that beautiful pink color.***

And now you know that whenever you want to, or you need to, you can easily remember this color (use the actual color if you know what it is), ***and you immediately return to this*** __________ (peaceful, joyful, loving, passionate, or whatever the client is seeking) ***state of being. Whenever you smell the fragrance of*** __________ (*Joy, or* whatever oil you are using), ***or even remember this fragrance, you immediately return to this state of*** _________(peaceful, joyful, loving, passionate, or whatever the client is seeking). ***No matter the time of day or night, no matter what the situation is, when you recall this beautiful color and fragrance you immediately return to that _______ state of being. It's so wonderful how easy it is for you to do this and so good to know that the more you do this, the easier it becomes.***

Now it's time to imagine a stairway of 5 steps, 5 steps that can take you back to the present time *of* ________ (insert today's day and date here).

Speaking in an energetic voice –

Counting back

and:

1; remembering everything you wish to remember from this time, clearly and easily

2; returning back into this present time of ________, feeling refreshed, relaxed and ready to use this wisdom in your present day life

3; feeling so very good about yourself, so good about who you are

4; beginning to stretch and move your arms and legs, to open and close your fingers

and

5; opening yours eyes and returning back fully present, fully awake and fully aware, remembering all that you wish to remember

Give the client a few moments to become fully awake and aware. Make sure that water is available and suggest that the client may feel like sharing part of this inner journey with you; or the client might prefer to keep quiet and process it later, at their own pace.

As a powerful tool for returning to this inner place and for remembering the information learned, the client may wish to obtain the essential oil used during the journey. If you have a supply on hand, you could give them a small sample to take away and practice with on their own. Remember to remind the client that this inner place can be accessed by them without the use of the oil.

Journey Into Inner Peace

With all the chaos in the outer world today it is no wonder that so many people are experiencing inner chaos, anxiety and stress. We would like to share this meditative inner journey and the oils that augment it with you. Of course, if you have your own meditation, yoga or prayer practice, you can utilize these same oils to enhance your experience.

Taking in a few deep breaths is a potent way to reduce stress and enhance wellness. Periodically throughout a busy day, I always recharge and take breathers with essential oils. Immediately, I sense the essential oils increasing oxygen to the cells and brain for better focus and productivity, enhancing my health and performance with an increased secretion of endorphins – for a greater sense of happiness and immune system support. What could be better? This is truly what we are looking for when we say that we *"need to take a breather."* A healthy practice of taking essential oil *breath-breaks* at work could enhance both productivity and worker's health and well-being. *Rosemary*, *Peppermint*, *Lavender*, and *Lemon* are all great for recharging when there's still work to be done, and my all time favorite may be the blend *En-R-Gee*. (Clients who wish to eliminate 'smoke breaks' are grateful to learn this strategy, too!)

One of the most favorite blends for creating inner peace is *Sacred Mountain* because its fragrance is that of nature, the forest and the deep peace that one finds in such a place. If you are new to the concept of energy, just take moment to close your eyes and imagine yourself driving in a traffic jam or in a crowded shopping mall... take a moment to notice how that feels in your body. Do you feel tightness anywhere? Anxiety, nervousness, impatience or frustration? Now shake that energy off and close your eyes once again, but this time imagine yourself standing or sitting in a beautiful forest, or maybe at the ocean shore... take a moment to feel this energy in your body, hear the sounds of a gentle breeze or the call of a bird in the distance. Do you feel a sense of peace and well-being? Maybe relaxation, and yes, even inner peacefulness? In our busy lives we may not be able to step out into nature every time we feel stressed or anxious, but we can take a few minutes to breathe in the fragrance of the oils that help to transport us to that inner, natural place of peace and relaxation. The following journey accents the oils, and on the other side of the same coin, the oils accent the journey. Each may be used independently, and together they harmonize, creating an even more powerful experience.

In addition to *Sacred Mountain* the following blends are also excellent for alchemically transforming the inner world from chaos into peace:

Peace and Calming – designed to promote relaxation and a deep sense of peace as well as release tension and uplift the spirit

Surrender – formulated to help surrender controlling attitudes and aggressive emotion; to release stress and tension

Gathering – helps overcome the bombardment of chaotic energy that takes us off our path of higher achievements and may help overcome stress, raise consciousness and bring about a feeling of peacefulness

Single oils recommended for this journey are:

German Chamomile – has an electrical frequency that promotes peace and harmony

Lavender – calming, relaxing and may bring about a sense of inner peace

Neroli – calms and relaxes, reduces anxiety and encourages a sense of joy and peace

Patchouli – calming and relaxing; reducing anxiety and bringing about a sense of peacefulness

Pine – helps sooth mental stress and relieve anxiety

Rose – helps bring balance and harmony and creates a sense of peace and well-being

Spruce – helps open and release emotional blocks bringing about a feeling of balance and of grounding.

Preparing for the Journey:

The following meditative journey script is written for the therapist to present to a client, but may easily be read and recorded so that it may be played back for personal use.

There are 3 parts to this journey:
The induction
The journey
The return to full awakened consciousness

Provide a comfortable, safe place where the client can sit or lie down in total relaxation. In preparing for this journey, make certain all electronic devices are turned off and that any potential distractions are removed. To ensure your client receives full benefit from this experience, plan approximately 45 to 60 minutes of undisturbed time. For a first time experience, there may be some normal hesitation or fear in letting go; a client who is already comfortable with the trance state may go much deeper. You may wish to make it clear that **the client** will control the pace during this safe process, and can go as deeply as they feel comfortable with.

Before the journey begins ask if it is OK to use the words *"Spirit Guides"* and/or *"Nature Devas"* with the client. I use Nature Devas for this journey out into nature, but you may use whatever is applicable to the client. This is to honor and respect that we are working with Divine Energy, the energy that heals. If these words are not OK with the client, take note of what words they would rather have you use.

Also, inform the client that during the journey you will allow them time to experience a feeling of deep inner peace and so as not to disturb this, you will wait quietly while they complete this process. Tell the client that when their process is complete, they will signal you by raising the index finger on one hand, to let you know that it is time to move on. Have the client establish this by raising that finger right now, so that later you will know which finger it will be.

When the client is in position, lying or sitting comfortably, invite the client to smell two or three single oils or blends and then tell you which one(s) they prefer you to use during their session.

Journey Into Inner Peace

Use a slow tempo with a soft, soothing voice throughout this induction. Instruct the client to close their eyes (if they have not already done so) and to take some nice deep breaths. The voice of the therapist is in bold font and italicized:

As you feel the breath enter and release from the body, you feel yourself sinking deeper into a place of peace and relaxation. During this time, you focus and observe the client's rising and falling chest, using the word ***"enter"*** as the client breathes in and ***"release"*** as the client exhales. This creates rapport, which helps the client to relax and go deeper.

After 3 – 5 deep breaths continue:

And now you might even begin to feel warm and gentle waves of relaxation beginning at the soles of your feet, to gently and slowly rise up through your ankles, up through the calves of your legs and into the knee joints. Each wave of relaxation helps you to let go and sink even deeper within... as these warm and gentle waves of relaxation rise into the muscles of the thighs and up through the groin, pelvis and buttocks, you allow yourself to relax even more. You might even feel a sense of peace as you let go and allow these waves of relaxation to rise into the abdomen, relaxing all the organs here and gently move into the lower back relaxing all the muscles there .... the waves of relaxation continue to move into the mid back, and into the upper back, relaxing, warming and soothing the muscles as they even fill the chest with warm relaxation, allowing

the heart to beat so easily and the lungs to breathe so effortlessly .... the waves of relaxation flow upwards through the neck and into the muscles of the jaw. You might even notice the jaw just drop ever so slightly as it fills with these comforting waves of relaxation ....as these warm waves fill the muscles of the cheeks and the muscles around the eyes with gentle relaxation you can even allow yourself to sink even deeper, and deeper as you may notice the eyelids becoming so heavy, so relaxed as these gentle waves rise up to the top of the head and even down into the brain itself, allowing the brain to relax and let go......

And here in this place you can even imagine a stairway of ten steps, a stairway of whatever kind you imagine, one that takes you down, down to a special place in nature; maybe one that you already know, or, maybe one that is new for you today. A sacred place where you can access that feeling of deep, inner, peace. It's so good to know that you can do this so easily, so effortlessly…

And now stepping onto step number 10, feeling the step beneath your foot as you allow yourself to sink even deeper...

and 9, knowing only that which is for your highest and greatest good can enter into this place ...

and 8, with each count you allow yourself to sink even deeper within ...

and 7, each step carrying you even deeper into that place of peace and inner wisdom...

and 6, calling here upon your Spirit Guides and Nature Devas, those who love you so dearly, who know your heart's desire to be here with you NOW, to guide you on this journey ...

as you sink even deeper ...

and 5 ...

and 4, feeling your own willingness to know what you may need to know, to release all energy that does not serve your highest good and to receive the gifts your guides have for you today ...

and 3, allowing all the cells of your body to open to memory and inner knowing

and 2 ... closer to that door or opening

and 1 ...

Stepping down ... now, onto the earth. Taking in a deep breath and feeling the earth beneath your feet as you begin to walk forward toward this sacred place in nature. As you step slowly along the path, you might even begin to sense how all the stress, anxiety and frustration (you can include any state of mind that the client is experiencing and wants to be free of in place or in addition to these) ***you have been carrying is beginning to move down and out of your body. You might even sense the color of this energy, and the weight of this energy as it begins to move down from the top of your head, down through all the muscles of the face ... down through the muscles of the neck and the shoulders, which, now free of this energy can relax and let go. It is so wonderful how with each step you take along this path you release even more of the tension you have been holding... with each breath you become more free and find it even easier to let go... easier to release all of that tension. You may even feel it releasing from your arms and hands... leaving your body and sinking deep into the earth as you walk along. Allowing the heaviness to release from your chest and abdomen, letting it go from the pelvis and groin... and letting it go from the muscles of the thighs, and the calves and from the feet... just letting it all disappear down into the earth to be transformed ...taking a deep breath and letting it all go ... now.***

You might even feel yourself getting a little lighter as you continue down this path to your sacred place. Maybe this place is deep within a forest or by the ocean shore, or maybe somewhere else, a place that is your special and private place in nature. Wherever it might be for you... you can reach that place, maybe now, or in a moment. You can find yourself there and allow yourself to find the perfect place to sit or to lie down, so relaxed, so comfortable.

Here the therapist can pass the cap from the bottle of the selected essential oil in front of the client's nostrils, slowly, several times, so that they take in the vibrational fragrance and energy of the single oil or blend, and while doing this, you say the following:

You might even smell the scent in the air, and that scent carries you even deeper within, deeper into that place of inner peace. You might hear the sounds around you, maybe the rustle of the wind, the song of a bird or the lapping of waves on the shore... who knows what sounds you will hear. You may even experience these sounds carrying you even deeper into that place of safety, peace and relaxation. So soft, and so relaxed, you might even sense the presence of the Nature Devas or your Spirit Guides around you... Who knows, you might even sense that they have a message for you, a message you can hear, now.

Stop and give the client one to two minutes for the message to come through, and then continue: ***And now you can even imagine the energy of peace surrounding you and within you. Breathe it into every cell of your body and sense if there is a color that symbolizes this inner peace. If there is, breathe this color deeply into your body, filling every cell of your body with this color.***

Continue to pass the cap of the essential oil or oil blend you are using in front of the client's nostrils at intervals all through this journey, even when the client is taking time in the sacred space.

Alternatively, ask the client to tell you if there is a color that they associate with this feeling of inner peace. This would be preferable, as it is more powerful to use their color. You would proceed this way:

Breathing the essential oil into every cell of your body you can sense if there is a color that symbolizes this deep, inner peace. If there is, you can speak that color aloud to me now. For example, if the color is green, you would say: ***That's right, breathe this beautiful green color of inner peace into every cell of your body. As you breathe in the scent in the air and absorb this beautiful color green*** (or naming the color if the client has told you) ***you can allow yourself to let go and sink even deeper into this place of sweet inner peace. You may stay here for as long as you wish, absorbing this inner peace into every cell of your being. And you can know that you can bring this feeling back with you into your present day life. But for now, just be here with this feeling, enjoying this inner peace, and, when you are ready, you can raise that finger and we will continue.*** Typically this will only take a few minutes, as time in this relaxed state seems much longer than it does in our awakened state. When the client moves the finger, continue on with:

That's right, its time to leave this sacred place now, but you know that you can return here anytime that you want to, any time that you need to. All you need to do is remember the color of inner peace and breathe it into your body, remember the scent in the air and you will feel the peace that you are feeling now. You might even take a moment to imagine yourself in a stressful situation, one that might have caused you to feel tension or frustration in the past, but now you just take in a deep breath and take one moment to focus on your color of peace and smell, or imagine your are smelling that scent in the air, take a deep breath and immediately you can feel our muscles relax, and find yourself back in this sacred place of inner peace. It's good to know that no matter what is happening around you, or who is there, you now know how to take yourself quickly, easily and effortlessly back into this place of inner

peace. And now that you have this new ability you are ready to return to your present day life:

Now you can easily imagine a stairway of 5 steps, 5 steps that can take you back to the present time *of* ________ (insert today's day and date here).

Speaking in an energetic voice –

Counting back

and:

1; remembering everything you wish to remember from this time, clearly and easily

2; returning back into this present time of _________, feeling refreshed, relaxed and ready to use this wisdom in your present day life

3; feeling so very good about yourself, so good about who you are

4; beginning to stretch and move your arms and legs, to open and close your fingers

and

5; opening yours eyes and returning back fully present, fully awake and fully aware, remembering all that you wish to remember

Give the client a few moments to become fully awake and aware. Make sure that water is available and suggest that the client may feel like sharing part of this inner journey with you; or the client might prefer to keep quiet and process it later, at their own pace.

As a powerful tool for returning to this inner place and for remembering the information learned, the client may wish to obtain the essential oil used during the journey. If you have a supply on hand, you could give them a small sample to take away and practice with on their own. Remember to remind the client that this inner place can be accessed by them without the use of the oil.

Inner Child Journey

The connection we have with our inner child often lies at the root of the challenges we face as adults, thus making it the most important relationship of our life, and yet often the most neglected. Many of us have been taught to put others first and are programmed into thinking that it is selfish to put our own wants and needs before those of others, especially the ones we love. All the energy we lavish on others in attempt to please them and obtain their love and acceptance so we feel like a good person, have a sense of belonging, and feel safe and secure, is really about our own inner child. Through Alchemical Hypnotherapy we can find this little child, rescue him or her from the past and bring that precious little one into the present time where we can provide new loving parents and all the love and acceptance that child has been longing for. Through this process we are able to rid ourselves of old, dysfunctional programs and write a new story for our life with our adult-self becoming the new and longed for parent of our own sweet inner child.

So how can essential oils help one to access and love the inner child? This is what Young Living has to say about their *Inner Child* special blend: *"Inner Child opens the pathway to connecting with the inner self that may have been damaged through childhood misuse or abuse. When children have been abused, they become disconnected from their natural identity, or inner child. This causes confusion and can contribute to undesirable personality traits. The sweet fragrance of this blend may stimulate memory response and help reconnect with the authentic self, which is one of the first steps toward finding emotional balance."* This is a wonderful blend for helping one to connect with the inner child and to begin to bring healing to the wounded inner child.

The *Inner Child* blend contains:

Orange: believed to stimulate joy, peace and happiness
Tangerine: calming, helping to relieve anxiety and nervousness

Jasmine: may help to relieve depression and nervous anxiety
Ylang Ylang: balances equilibrium and restores confidence and self-love
Sandalwood: high in sesquiterpenes which stimulates the pineal gland and limbic region of the brain; the center of our emotions
Spruce: helps open and release emotional blocks
Lemongrass: may increase the flow of oxygen and uplift the spirit
Neroli: highly regarded by the Egyptians for healing and calming the mind, body and spirit. It is said to be strengthening to the emotions and supports inner peace, confidence and awareness.

The blend *Joy* promotes a feeling of love and happiness in the inner child, a blend that promotes peace and calming is appropriately named *Peace and Calming*. Either of these essential oil blends are good choices for this meditative inner journey. If you don't have these blends you might use the uplifting oil of *Orange or Lemongrass* (see above).

If while doing this meditative journey feelings of anger or memory trauma of the past surfaces, the client should be advised to make an appointment with an experienced Alchemical Hypnotherapist or other professional who specializes in Inner Child work. (See **Post Inner Child Journey Notes** on page 86.)

For readers who are trained in Inner Child work, the essential oil blends that may help to release anger and memory of trauma that is locked in the cells of the body are:

Release: The fragrance of *Release* may help to bring about a feeling of freedom, while rubbing a few drops of the blend over the area of the liver may help to release old trauma and support a sense of peace and well being.

Sara: An oil blend specifically designed to help relax the mind and encourage release of sexual and/or ritual abuse. This blend may also help to unlock physical and emotional abuse as well. The fragrant influences of *Sara* are said to

bring peace and freedom to the soul so that moving on in life with freedom becomes possible.

Trauma Life: An oil blend created to support the release of buried emotional trauma. This is a soothing, calming and grounding blend that helps release the trauma and stress caused by fatigue and anger that is carried into the present from past traumatic experiences.

Young Living provides a wide variety of oil blends created with the intention of supporting physical, emotional, mental and spiritual healing. These blends are too numerous to list here, but if you are interested in learning more about the different oils and oil blends offered by YL, please visit our website.

Preparing for the Journey:

The following meditative journey script is written for the hypnotherapist to present to a client, but may easily be read and recorded so that it may be played back for personal use. Please read the Post Inner Child Journey Notes at the end of this chapter before proceeding.

There are 3 parts to this journey:
The induction
The journey
The return to full awakened consciousness

Provide a comfortable, safe place where the client can sit or lie down in total relaxation. In preparing for this journey, make certain all electronic devices are turned off and that any potential distractions are removed. To ensure your client receives full benefit from this experience, plan approximately 45 to 60 minutes of undisturbed time. For a first time experience, there may be some normal hesitation or fear in letting go; a client who is already comfortable with the trance state may go much deeper. You may wish to make it clear that **the client** will control the pace during this safe process, and can go as deeply as they feel comfortable with.

Before the journey begins who or what the client connects with in the Divine realm. This could be God, Jesus, Buddha, Muhammad, a Power Animal, Holy Angel or any type of Spirit Guide. We do this to honor and respect Divine Energy as the energy that heals. The inner Child is actually a guide to our Spiritual Guides, and often those who are holding onto childhood traumas are unable to connect with the spiritual guidance they seek because the wounded child blocks that communication. When the inner child is honored, embraced and loved, the adult often finds his or her heart and third eye open more fully to Divine energy and guidance. The inner child, just the same as an outer child, is fully connected to God or Divine Energy.

Also, inform the client that during the journey they will have an opportunity to experience a feeling of deep inner peace, and that you will wait quietly while they complete this process. Tell the client that when their process is complete, they will signal you by raising the index finger on one hand, to let you know that it is time to move on. Have the client establish this by raising that finger right now, so that later you will know which finger it will be. There will also be a time during the journey when you will ask whether the inner child greets the client, or if the inner child holds back. To do this, establish a "yes" and "no" finger prior to starting the journey. Ask the client to show you which finger will be used for a "yes" answer, and which for the "no" answer.

Ask the client "What are the things that you wished your mother, father, grandparents, teachers or other significant adults in your life would have told you when you were a child?" Make a list of these things in the client's *exact* words, as you will need them toward the end of this journey.

The *Inner Child* blend is most conducive to this journey, but if not available, you may offer the client a choice of two or three essential oil blends or single oils that you have on hand. Explain the properties of each and ask which one the client prefers you to use. When the client is in position, lying or sitting comfortably, instruct him or her to close their eyes and take in some nice deep, relaxing breaths. Use a slow tempo with a soft, soothing voice throughout this induction.

Inner Child Journey

In this script the voice of the therapist is bold font and italicized:

As you feel the breath enter and release from the body, you feel yourself sinking deeper into a place of peace and relaxation. During this time focus on the client's chest and use the word ***"enter"*** as the client breathes in and ***"release"*** as the client exhales. This creates rapport, which helps the client to relax and go deeper.

After 3 – 5 deep breaths continue:

And now you might even begin to feel warm and gentle waves of relaxation beginning at the soles of your feet beginning to gently and slowly rise up through your ankles, the calves of your legs and into the knee joints. Each wave of relaxation helps you to let go and sink even deeper within... as these warm and gentle waves of relaxation rise into the muscles of the thighs and up through the groin, pelvis and buttocks, you allow yourself to relax even more. You might even feel as sense of peace as you let go and allow these waves of relaxation to rise into the abdomen, relaxing all the organs here and gently move into the lower back relaxing all the muscles here... the waves of relaxation continue to move into the mid-back, and into the upper back, relaxing, warming and soothing the muscles as they even fill the chest with warm relaxation, allowing the heart to beat so easily and the lungs to breathe so effortlessly... the waves of relaxation flow upwards through the neck and into the muscles of the jaw. You might even notice the jaw just drop ever so slightly as it fills with these comforting waves of relaxation... as these warm waves fill the muscles of the cheeks and the muscles around the eyes with gentle relaxation you can even allow your self to sink even deeper, and deeper. You may even notice the eyelids becoming so heavy, so relaxed as these gentle waves rise up to the top of the head and even down into the brain itself, allowing the brain to relax and let go...

And here in this place you can even imagine a stairway of ten steps, a stairway of whatever kind you imagine, one that takes you down, down to a very special place where today, very soon, you can meet that little child who lives within… That precious little one who is longing for you to come, that sweet little one who is most treasured by you. It's so good to know that you can do this so easily, so effortlessly...

And now stepping onto step number 10, feeling the step beneath your foot as you allow yourself to sink even deeper...

and 9, knowing only that which is for your highest and greatest good can enter into this place ...

and 8, with each count you allow yourself to sink even deeper within ...

and 7, each step carrying you even deeper into that place of peace and inner wisdom...

and 6, calling here upon** (whomever your client wishes you to all upon) **and all those who love you so dearly and who know your heart's desire to connect with your inner child to be here with you NOW, to guide you on this journey ...

as you sink even deeper ...

and 5 ...

and 4, feeling your own willingness to know what you may need to know, to release all energy that does not serve your highest good and to receive the gifts your guides have for you today ...

and 3, allowing all the cells of your body to open to memory and inner knowing

and 2 ... closer to that very special place

and 1 ...

Stepping down off that last step and finding yourself in a very special place...a place where you can meet your little inner child...Take a moment now to breathe in and become aware of what this place is like. It might be a room or somewhere out in nature...wherever it is, know that it is the perfect place for you and your child to meet. Take a moment now to become even more aware of this place as you begin to sense the energy of this little child. At this point the hypnotherapist can pass the cap from the essential oil in front of the client's nostrils; continue to do this at intervals during the session.

Maybe this little one is there, ready to greet you ... or maybe your inner child is shy, or maybe even afraid. Gently allow yourself all the time you need to make a connection with that precious child. Here you can ask the client: ***Does the little child come running to meet you*?** If the client responds with the "**yes**" finger, move on to Journey A, while if the "**no**" finger is lifted go to Journey B.

Journey A:
That's right she *(or he, use the appropriate pronoun for the client)* ***is so happy that you are here. You may want to reach down and pick this child up with a hug and tell this little one how happy you are to be here today. Just take a moment to feel that little one's body close to yours and feel the love you have for this precious little child...*** Give the client a minute or so to have this experience. ***Now look into the eyes of this child...your child, and tell this child all the wonderful things that you love about her*** (or him*).* Give the client a few moments of silence to do this.

Now you can invite this little one to take you by the hand and show you something, maybe something that the child wants you to see so that you can understand a challenge that you are experiencing ... or maybe this child wants to take you to meet a very special Spiritual Guide, one who can answer your questions ... you can take the child's

hand, letting this little one lead you to where he (she) wants you to go. Just raise the finger on your hand to signal me when you are there.

After seeing the finger rise, the therapist continues: ***That's right, now you can easily know and experience what this child wants you to know. Take all the time you need and again raise that finger when you are ready to move on.***

Again after seeing the finger rise, the therapist carries on: ***That's right; now that your little child has shared this with you, you can bring this information and understanding back with you into your daily, waking life.***

You can take a moment now to thank that little child for meeting here with you. And ask if there is anything more that the child wants you to know? Is there anything needed from you before you leave this place?

Give the client a few moments for this, and then say: ***Take a moment now to look into the eyes of this precious child.*** At this time the therapist reads the list of things the client wanted to hear as a child. Read slowly and with feeling. You may want to read the list over 3 or 4 times, changing the order as you do so.

And now you might even invite this special child into your heart, so that this child is always present with you. Let this child know that you are always here and that you love her (him) ***very dearly ... that this little one is most precious in your life. Just allowing that sweet little one to sink deep within your heart, NOW. And every time you touch your heart or even think of your heart, you remember this little child ... your little child who is so special to you. Every time you look at your self in the mirror you see that precious little child in the reflection in your eyes and you send love and joy to that little one. You feel so happy, so grateful to share this love with your little inner child.*** Of course in saying this, the client is affirming that the most precious one in their life is themselves. Remember to pass the cap of the *Inner Child* blend, or whichever oil you are using, in front of the client's nostrils at this time to deepen the experience.

Journey B:

If the client responds with a "No", follow this protocol:

That's right, maybe this little one is hiding or standing back. Maybe your inner child is afraid to come close to you right now, and that is OK. You can let this little child know that you understand about the hurt in the past and that you have come into this place today to bring love and comfort. Letting that child know that you will wait right here and if at any time this little child feels comfortable enough to come to you, you will reach out a hand, that you will give that little child a hug or whatever is needed. Let this little one know that while maybe, in the past, you have not been here for them, now you are... maybe you want to tell this little one that you are sorry for how this child was treated in the past, but now you know differently, now you are learning and growing and realize how very important and special this little child is to you. Give the client a few quiet moments here to be in this energy with their child.

And now you can look into the eyes of this little one and say the things that you want this child to know. You might even imagine sending love out from your heart to the heart of this little one as you express these feelings. Give the client a minute or so with their inner child at this time.

And now be aware and sense how this little inner child may be even a little more open to you, who knows, maybe now this little one is ready to take your hand, or maybe is already in your arms ... just take a moment to be with this child in whatever way the child wants you to be. Let this sweet little one know how precious they are to you, as together you listen to these words ... listen and breathe in the energy of these words, now.

At this time the hypnotherapist reads the list of things the client wanted to hear as a child. Read slowly and with feeling. You may want to read the list over 3 or 4 times, changing the order as you do so.

You can take a moment now to thank that little child for meeting here with you. And ask if there is anything more that the child wants you to know? Is there anything needed from you before you leave this place? Just let this child know that you are here now for them. You might even invite this little one to come inside your heart, or if the child is not ready to do that, maybe there is a special place close by where this child can be. Let this little one know that you will come back, to meet again, soon.

Let this child know that you love her (him) very dearly … that he (or she) ***is now becoming the most precious one in your life. Every time you look at your self in the mirror you see that precious little child in the reflection in your eyes and you send love and joy to that little one. You feel so happy, so grateful to share this love with your little inner child. And every night as you drift off to sleep you remember this little child, sending love and acceptance.*** Of course in saying this, the client is affirming that the most precious one in their life is their self. Remember to pass the cap of the *Inner Child* blend, or whichever oil you are using, in front of the client's nostrils at this time to deepen the experience.

After completing Journey A or Journey B:

And now it's time to leave this special place, but now you have that precious little child safe nearby or within your heart, and as you breathe in the scent of the Inner Child essential oil (or other oil), ***you can easily, effortlessly feel all the love you have for that child. And now,***

You can easily imagine a stairway of 5 steps, 5 steps that can take you back to the present time of ________ (insert today's day and date here).

Speaking in an energetic voice –

Counting back

and:

1; remembering everything you wish to remember from this time, clearly and easily

2; returning back into this present time of ________, feeling refreshed, relaxed and ready to use this wisdom in your present day life

3; feeling so very good about yourself, so good about who you are

4; beginning to stretch and move your arms and legs, to open and close your fingers

and

5; opening yours eyes and returning back fully present, fully awake and fully aware, remembering all that you wish to remember

Give the client a few moments to become fully awake and aware. Make sure that water is available and suggest that the client may feel like sharing part of this inner journey with you; or the client might prefer to keep quiet and process it later, at their own pace.

As a powerful tool for returning to this inner place and for remembering the information learned, the client may wish to obtain the essential oil used during the journey. If you have a supply on hand, you could give them a small sample to take away and practice with on their own. Fragrance is a powerful tool for activating memories, and though it does work to return back into the memory connected with it, also remember to remind the client of this most precious inner child and that the feeling of love may be easily accessed without the use of the oil.

Post Inner Child Journey Notes:

This journey can be profoundly powerful; the hypnotherapist must be sensitive to the needs of the client. If the client answered "yes" to the child coming forward at the beginning of the journey, that is an indication that the client already has a healthy relationship, or at minimum has begun to form a healthy relationship, with their inner child. If however the answer to this question is a "no", the hypnotherapist needs to be aware that past memories of trauma and/or abuse may surface during the session. Remember that it is OK for the client to cry and feel these memories, however if the client appears to be in distress, you may wish to say; ***"Yes, this child has experienced difficult things that you are now remembering but now you are here in*** *(give the place, date and year)* ***and that you and your child are protected and in a safe place now."*** This should bring calm to the client as it reminds the client that this is only a memory and this is today and that they are in a safe place with you now.

You can check in with the client at the end of the session to learn how meeting with their child was for them. If it was traumatic in any way, ask if the response of the child was different at the end of the journey than it was at the beginning. If the child was more open at the end, then you know progress was made and that taking the client on another journey like this in a week or so will most probably bring even more positive results. If there was no difference, or if the child retreated even further, the client should be counseled to make an appointment with an experienced Alchemical Hypnotherapist or other professional who specializes in Inner Child work. Make sure that the client is feeling reassured and fully in the present before leaving your office.

Homework that is beneficial to give clients as a follow-up to this journey:

- Keep a journal of thoughts, feelings or memories that may surface following this experience.

- Each morning as you look in the mirror, take a moment to look into your eyes and think of your little child with feelings of love and happiness.

- At night just before dropping off to sleep, think of this little one and express how precious and special this child is to you. If appropriate, imagine holding this little one in your arms as you drop off to sleep.

- Keep your bottle of the essential blend *Inner Child* (or other oil that you are using) with you and breathe in the fragrance whenever you feel stressed, sad, angry or just want to connect with your inner child. The fragrant scent will immediately stimulate memories of the journey and of the sweetness of your inner child. Remember, the fragrance of the oils goes straight to the limbic system of the brain and thus stimulates memory and emotion to make the connection with your inner child even more powerful and sweet.

- Remember that whatever your inner dialogue is about yourself, you are saying that to your precious little inner child. Would you rather choose to speak more kindly, or is what you really want to say to your inner child? This is very important as it takes time to change old habits and the inner child needs to know that you are making changes. Instead of thinking critical thoughts like: *"You were so stupid to do that!"* change to *"You are so smart and it's OK; everyone does silly things sometime."* Or, *"You are so smart and it's OK, everyone makes mistakes."*

As your client practices on a daily basis, their relationship with their inner child will improve - and their life will improve. Remember, using essential oils with the homework deepens and strengthens this process.

Journey to the Future Self

The intention of this guided inner journey, is for the recipient to receive advice and inspiration by journeying to their Future Self. Many people today are stressed about the future. If you or your client is having difficulty choosing a course or sticking to a path, this journey can be very helpful. This is an excellent way to find information about avoiding unnecessary bumps in the road, to find the best breezes for your sails, to place yourself in a good position to receive everything you need. When we have decisions to make, it's good to research and consult with best friends, spiritual counselors, expert professionals, parents, siblings and elders. Within each of us is another excellent resource - your very own Future Self. Hindsight is a wonderful thing!

Frankincense will help to visualize while remaining centered. The blend *Into The Future* may engage your client's pioneering spirit to embark on this journey. *Dreamcatcher* enhances positive visualization and the realization of desires on the path to fulfillment. Another favorite choice for this journey is *Transformation*, a blend containing *Lemon, Peppermint, Sandalwood, Frankincense* and *Rosemary*. And to enhance access to inner vision, a drop of *Awaken* rubbed clockwise over the center of the forehead may awaken the third eye. Invite your client to help choose the essential oil for their journey.

The following journey script is written for the hypnotherapist to present to a client, but may easily be read and recorded and played back later for personal use.

Preparing for the Journey:

Inform the client that during the journey there will be an opportunity to make a deep connection with their Future Self. Their Future Self will look like them (of course!) only older, will be very loving, and extremely pleased to see them. At the appropriate time, you will wait quietly while the client has this experience. When the connection with the Future Self has completed, the client will need to signal you by raising the index finger on one hand, to let you know that it is time to move on and return to the present. Have the client establish this by raising that finger right now, so that later you will know which finger it will be.

There are 3 parts to this journey:
The induction
The journey
The return to full awakened consciousness

Provide a comfortable, safe place where the client can sit or lie down in total relaxation. In preparing for this journey, make certain all electronic devices are turned off and that any potential distractions are removed. To ensure your client receives full benefit from this experience, plan approximately 45 to 60 minutes of undisturbed time. For a first time experience, there may be some normal hesitation or fear in letting go; a client who is already comfortable with the trance state may go much deeper. You may wish to make it clear that **the client** will control the pace during this safe process, and can go as deeply as they feel comfortable with.

When the client is in position, ask if you may rub one drop of *Awaken* (or *Frankincense*) on the centre of their forehead. With their permission, you then place a drop on your finger and gently rub it onto the forehead, spreading the oil in clockwise circles with the intention of opening the third eye. Then, pass your fingers under the client's nostrils to engage the olfactory sense.

Journey to the Future Self

Use a slow tempo with a soft, soothing voice throughout this induction. Instruct the client to close their eyes (if they have not already done so) and to take some nice deep, relaxing breaths. The voice of the therapist is in bold font and italicized:

As you feel the breath enter and gently release from the body, you feel yourself completely relaxing, allowing the chair (or bed) to completely support you, sinking deeply inside now, into a place of total peace... quiet, and relaxation. During this time, you focus and observe the client's rising and falling chest, saying ***"enter"*** as the client breathes in and ***"release"*** as the client exhales. This creates rapport, which helps the client to relax and go deeper.

After 3 – 5 deep breaths continue:

Good...And now you might even begin to feel warm and gentle waves of relaxation beginning at the soles of your feet, to gently and slowly rise up through your ankles, up through the calves of your legs and into the knee joints. Each wave of relaxation helps you to let go and sink even deeper into relaxation...and peace... and as these warm and gentle waves of relaxation rise into the muscles of the thighs and up through the groin, pelvis and buttocks, you allow yourself to relax even more. You might even feel a sense of peace as you let go and allow these waves of relaxation to rise into the abdomen, relaxing all the organs here and gently move into the lower back relaxing all the muscles here .... the waves of relaxation continue to move into the mid back, and into the upper back, relaxing, warming and soothing the muscles as they even fill the chest with warm relaxation, allowing the heart to beat so easily and the lungs to breathe so effortlessly .... the waves of relaxation flow upwards through the neck and into the muscles of the jaw. You might even notice the jaw just drop ever so slightly as it fills with these comforting waves of relaxation ....as these warm waves fill the muscles of the cheeks and the muscles around the eyes with gentle relaxation you can even allow yourself to sink even deeper, and deeper as you may notice the eyelids becoming so heavy, so relaxed as these gentle waves rise up to the top of the head and even down into the brain itself, allowing the brain to relax and let go......

And here in this peace and relaxation you can even imagine a stairway of ten steps, a stairway of whatever kind you imagine, one that takes you down, down to a very special place where today, very soon, you can meet with your Future Self... a part of you who loves you dearly and

who is SO happy to meet with you today.. It's so good to know that you can do this so easily, so effortlessly...

And now stepping onto step number 10, feeling the step beneath your foot as you allow yourself to sink even deeper...

and 9, knowing only that which is for your highest and greatest good can enter into this peace ...

and 8, with each count you allow yourself to sink even deeper within ...

and 7, each step carrying you even deeper into that place of peace and inner wisdom...

and 6, calling here upon your inner wisdom and all those guides who love you so dearly and who know your heart's desire to connect with your Future Self to be here with you NOW, to guide you on this journey ...

as you sink even deeper ...

and 5 ...

and 4, feeling your own willingness to learn what you may need to know, to release all energy that does not serve your highest good and to receive the gifts your Future Self has for you today ...

and 3, allowing all the cells of your body to open to inner knowing

and 2 ... closer to that very special place

and 1 ...

Stepping down off that last step and finding yourself in a very special place...a place where you can meet your Future Self... Take a moment now to breathe in and become aware of what this place is like. It might be a

room, or somewhere out in nature...wherever it is, know that it is the perfect place for you and your Future Self to meet. Take a moment now to become even more aware of this place as you begin to sense the energy of your Future Self coming forward to greet you. At this point the hypnotherapist can pass the cap from the essential oil in front of the client's nostrils; continue to do this at intervals during the session. ***And, taking a moment now to greet your Future Self, gently allowing your Future Self to guide you to an inner room or place of sanctuary in their life, where you can talk easily, and ask your questions... You may wish to ask whether there is anything you can do right now or tomorrow to make the path easier, or how best to place yourself in life in order to get everything you need. Perhaps your Future Self will show you in pictures, or tell you with words... everything that you need to know... I will wait quietly now. When you are complete, you can move your finger to signal me that it is time to move on.***
Quietly wait for the client to move their finger. If sufficient time has passed and there is no finger movement you may suggest that ***maybe now or in a moment you will know that it is time to move on and that finger will signal to me.***

After the signal:
And yes, now it is time to leave this place, knowing that you can return here any time you wish to.... You may like to ask your Future Self now, if there is anything more that they want to share with you, or if there is a gift they have for you. Wait for a moment, then go on: ***If there is a gift, you can sense and know its purpose. You can take this gift and all the wisdom that you have gained and place it in your body, maybe in or near to your heart or any place which is right for you. . I will wait a moment while you do this...*** Wait for a moment, then go on: ***And you know that you can access this gift at any time just by remembering it here within you, or by gently touching this place on your body.***

Now... it is time to say goodbye and to thank your Future Self for all that they have shared with you today. Now it's time to imagine a stairway of 5 steps, 5 steps that can take

you back to the present time and place of _______(today's date and your location.)

Speaking in an energetic voice –

Counting back

and:

1; remembering everything you wish to remember from this journey, clearly and easily

2; returning back into this present time of ________, feeling refreshed, relaxed and ready to use this wisdom in your present day life

3; feeling so very good about yourself, so good about who you are

4; beginning to stretch and move your arms and legs, to open and close your fingers

and

5; opening yours eyes and returning back fully present, fully awake and fully aware, remembering all that you wish to remember!

Give the client a few moments to become fully awake and aware. Make sure that water is available and suggest that the client may feel like sharing part of this inner journey with you; or the client might prefer to keep quiet and process it later, at their own pace.

As a powerful tool for returning to this inner place and for remembering the information learned, the client may wish to obtain the essential oil used during the journey. If you have a supply on hand, you could give them a small sample to take away and practice with on their own. Remember to remind the client that this inner place can be accessed by them without the use of the oil.

The Abundance Ritual

By Linda Baker

We are on this planet to enjoy and partake of all the wonderfulness around us, and abundance allows us to fully enjoy and participate in life. Abundance is expressed in many ways and to live a fully abundant life we need a balance of all forms of abundance. There is **material abundance** that expresses itself through physical things, money and the freedom it gives us, including the ability to attend the classes, workshops and events that we desire. **Health abundance** allows us the capability to do the things we want to do, to care for our health and to eat, drink and supplement our bodies with healthy things. **Emotional abundance** allows us to live in a balanced emotional state, while **educational abundance** is the abundance to learn and enrich our lives. **Relationship abundance** is the supply of loving people who care for us and whom we care about. When our life is filled with balanced abundance we are more likely to live in a joy-filled, generous and compassionate way.

There have been numerous things written on creating abundance, attracting wealth and gaining prosperity and while I have used several tools in the arena, I find that combining a few key ingredients with the use of Young Living's essential oil blend of *Abundance* was, and is, fundamental to the joyful abundance that I live today.

When I purchased my first bottle of YL oil over twenty years ago, I never would have dreamed to own the large collection of oils that grace the shelves of my healing room today. Back then it seemed that I would never be able to afford them, and even when I decided to purchase the oil blend of *Abundance* for $26 (the price back then) I felt a tightness in my stomach and a inner dread that it was a foolish mistake to spend so much for such a small bottle of oil. That fear could have not been further from the truth. With the commitment to use the oil blend of *Abundance* every day, I noticed that my life was changing. It happened slowly and quietly, but after a few months I was earning more money and had more money to purchase the oils that I had come to love. It seemed almost magical how my thoughts and energy shifted so that not only was I buying *Abundance* for myself, but also I was giving sample bottles to students. It seemed that the more I gave, the more my oil collection began to grow. Slowly, organically, all the areas of abundance began to open in my life. I felt happier, was freer and noticed how much I was enjoying the life I was living! My life is greatly blessed with great abundance now and using and sharing Young Living essential oils is a big part of this wonderful transformation!

All this is precisely why I have chosen to include in this book my personal ritual for abundance, created for using the essential oil blend of *Abundance* – I want to share all I have learned about attracting abundance with you and I want you to have the tools you need to live an abundant life now. To enhance this already powerful stand alone ritual, I have created a special meditative journey called "*The Journey Into Abundance"*, available as a free mp3 download when you purchase a bottle of *Abundance* blend through our website. To learn how to receive this valuable free gift, please see the next section of this book, "Where to get therapeutic grade essential oils for your practice".

First: Please note that somatides transmit frequency through fragrance and the thought process. About the essential oil blend of *Abundance* from *The Peoples Desk Reference for Essential Oils,* 1999 edition:

> *This blend was created to enhance the frequency of the energy field that surrounds us through the electrical stimulation of the somatides. Somatides transmit the frequency from the cells to the outside of the body when they are stimulated through fragrance and the thought process. This frequency, called the electrical field or the aura, creates what is called the "law of attraction," or that which we attract to ourselves. This might bring about an abundance of health, both physical and emotional. The oils in Abundance also contain tremendous antiviral and antifungal properties.*

For this abundance ritual we are directing the thought process to full abundance with a specific intention on financial abundance.

The YL essential oil blend of *Abundance* contains 8 individual oils. These are the oils of *Myrrh, Cinnamon Bark, Frankincense, Patchouli, Orange, Ginger, Clove* and *Spruce*.

The essential oil of *Myrrh* has one of the highest levels of sesquiterpenes (a class of compounds that has a direct effect on the hypothalamus, pituitary and amygdala, the emotional center of the brain) and has been used throughout the ages in eastern countries to enhance spiritual awareness. It is also said that the oil of *Myrrh* has the frequency of wealth.

The essential oil of *Cinnamon Bark* is known as the oil of wealth from the Orient, and thought to possess the frequency that attracts wealth and abundance.

The essential oil of *Frankincense*, valued more than gold in ancient times, is the holy anointing oil. It is rich in sesquiterpenes that help oxygenate the pineal and pituitary glands, so to elevate the mind and relieve depression and despair.

The essential oil of *Patchouli* is reported in legends to represent money and those who possessed it were considered wealthy.

The essential oil of *Orange* contains a frequency that is said to elevate the mind and body to bring about feelings of joy, peace and happiness.

The essential oil of *Clove* is associated with great abundance in the Orient. It is said that to possess the oil of clove was to possess wealth.

The essential oil of *Ginger* is gentle and stimulating, assisting with strength and courage.

The essential oil of *Spruce* has a fragrance that helps to open and release emotional blocks bringing about a feeling of

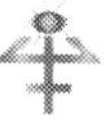

balance and grounding. It is also said to possess the frequency of prosperity.

In the above I focused upon the vibrational frequencies of the oils that support the attraction of abundance, but it is important to note that all of these oils in lesser and greater ways support the physical health and well-being of the body as well. Most of these oils contain antibacterial, antifungal and antiviral properties. As physical health is important to balanced abundance, these oils are of immense value in this arena as well as in raising the frequency of the electric field, or aura.

The Peoples Desk Reference for Essential Oils, 1999 edition explains the fragrant influence of the essential oil blend of *Abundance*:

When focusing on issues of abundance and inhaling this oil, a memory link to the RNA template is created where the memory is blueprinted and then passed to and stored in the DNA memory bank. Then every time you smell the oil the mental energy for abundance is created. The frequency of this blend is believed to create a harmonic magnetic energy field around oneself.

In a quick review of the individual oils contained in the blend of *Abundance* we can see that all the aspects required for attracting abundance are present. *Spruce* assists with opening and releasing blockages that get in the way of our feeling deserving of and allowing abundance to enter our lives, while the oil of *Ginger* supports our courage to move into the new frequency of abundance. Whenever we move from our comfortable frequency to one of higher vibration, feelings of resistance, fear, and or guilt may arise. Often our old beliefs and programming cause us to believe it is not right for us to desire or attract greater abundance in our lives. The oils of *Orange* and *Frankincense* help to elevate the mind and raise our vibrational energy to a higher frequency that is more receptive to receiving abundance, while the oils of *Cinnamon*, *Myrrh*, *Clove* and *Patchouli* all contain the frequency of abundance and wealth. The synergy created by this combination of individual oils results in a blend that truly assists the user to release blockages and

open to receiving, attracting and possessing balanced abundance.

The Abundance Ritual

Every morning follow this routine. If you take a morning shower or bath, do this afterwards, as you will not want to wash away the oils after the treatment.

Sit down and place 2 – 3 drops of the *Abundance* blend onto the palm of one hand. Bring the index finger of the opposite hand down through the auric field (starting at approximately 12 – 18 inches above the palm) and make 3 clockwise circles in the oil. This simple process helps increase the vibrational frequency of the oil. (See page 14.) In some spiritual teachings the index finger is considered to be the *"chi finger,"* and using it releases the most potent chi. Rub the oil into the sole of your foot.

The pores of the soles of the feet are the largest in the body, and that which is rubbed into them permeates the entire body within a short time. While doing this, hold the intention for all blocks that keep you from attracting the abundance you desire in your life be dissolved and state that you are open to receiving abundance now.

You can make this even more powerful by speaking the words out loud and by being specific about the abundance you are open to and ready to bring into your life. For example, you might say something like, *"I am now open to receiving financial wealth,"* or, *"I am now open to my body having all the energy it needs to do the things I love."* If you find that your mind is resisting your words and intentions, add a clause such as this to your statement: *"I am now open to receiving financial wealth, even though I don't think I deserve it"* or, *"I am now open to my body having all the energy it needs to do the things I love, even though I don't understand how it can happen".* The "even though" statement needs to be a statement of what your mind is saying when it fights against your stated intention. Take a moment to feel the energy in your body when you state your desire without the "even though" statement, and then, how it feels when you do. If you feel resistance to the statement of your intention, by including the "even though" statement you should feel that resistance decrease and dance **with** your intention, rather than fight against it.

After this, you can rub *Young Living Rose Ointment* over the *Abundance* blend to seal it in so that it is longer lasting, and then put on your sock. If you do not have *Rose Ointment*, you may use a natural, unscented cream in its place.

Repeat the above with the other foot and you are ready to go on with your day.

Do this ritual in the morning and if you would like even more energy to create abundance in your life, repeat this entire process before you go to sleep each night. Enjoy this for at least 30 days as it has been shown that it takes this much time to change a habit. The habit you are changing is your vibrational abundance frequency setting.

Please remember that feelings or thoughts may come up that seem contrary to attracting abundance as you continue to do this abundance ritual. If and when they do, instead of trying to suppress them, welcome them. They are coming forward to be recognized and healed. Remember to use the "even though" statement with these thoughts. For example if a thought says: *"this will not work for you,"* instead of giving it power, simply say *"I choose abundance, even though part of me believes this will not work for me."* Notice how it feels to say this, to know you are choosing abundance and that you don't have to fully believe it now in order to move in that direction.

If you have purchased a bottle of *Abundance* through our website, after you complete the abundance ritual would be a good time to listen to the *"The Journey Into Abundance"* meditative journey. If you do the abundance ritual at bedtime and then listen to the meditative journey before falling to sleep, your subconscious mind will focus on attracting abundance into your life as you sleep.

If old programming continues to block you from feeling abundant and from attracting abundance in any form into your life, consider doing deeper trance work with a trained Alchemical Hypnotherapist.

On our website www.alchemicalscents.com you can learn how to contact an Alchemical therapist.

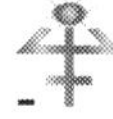

Creating a Sacred Healing Space

Vibrational energy exists everywhere, so whether your healing space is for personal use, for receiving clients, or both, you want an atmosphere that is physically and energetically clean and clear as well as one that carries an uplifting and sacred vibration. One of the best ways to create such a space is through diffusing pure essential oils.

Diffusing Essential Oils

Diffused oils create a pleasant aroma in addition to increasing oxygen availability in the air and producing negative ions. When this is done the healing aspects of the oils can enter our olfactory system and stimulate the limbic lobe, or emotional center of our brain.

For best results use a cold-air diffuser as dispersing the oils in this manner preserves their therapeutic properties. A cold-air diffuser atomizes a micro-fine mist of essential oils into the air where they can remain suspended for several hours. Research has shown that cold-air diffusing of certain oils has many positive effects, including these:

- Reduce bacteria, mold, fungus and unpleasant odors
- Relax the mind and relieve tension
- Clear the mind while improving concentration and alertness
- Stimulate neurotransmitters
- Stimulate spiritual awareness and sensitivity
- Promote deep meditation

Today there is much concern about viruses, airborne bacteria and other microbes that cause infections. Keeping your healing room as well as yourself protected is important for your health as well as for your client's well being. What do you do when someone comes in with a cold or cough, or feels like he or she is "coming down with something"?

Diffusing Young Living oil blends of *Thieves* or *Purification* may be the answer. In 1997 the *Thieves* oil blend was tested at Weber State University for its potent antimicrobial properties and was found to have a 99.96 percent kill rate against airborne bacteria. Diffusing *Thieves* for 15 to 30 minutes every 3 to 4 hours, helps keep the air in your room free of airborne bacteria.

The antiseptic blend of *Purification* was formulated for diffusing, to clean the air and neutralize mildew, cigarette smoke and disagreeable odors. Diffuse for 15 to 30 minutes every 3 to 4 hours to purify the space.

Diffusing essential oils is a wonderful way to prepare your room to receive a client. To name a few of the positive effects, a light fragrance of the oils in the air assists in creating a healing space by promoting relaxation, reducing anxiety, stimulating memories, lending a feeling of courage, and increasing spiritual awareness. Remember that even people who are sensitive to smells are most often open to pure essential oils. However, when you are scheduling the session you may wish to ask if your client is open to the diffusing of essential oils to augment the session.

For best results, diffuse all oils in a cold-air diffuser for 10 to 15 minutes before your client arrives. Here are some examples of client issues for which diffusing essential oils may be helpful:

For grief over the loss of a relationship or of a loved one, you might diffuse the oil of *Cypress,* as the fragrant influence of this oil eases the feeling of loss and creates a sense of security and grounding.

For a depressed, hopeless or stressed client you may choose to diffuse the oils of:

> *Geranium* as its fragrant influence helps to release negative memories, ease nervous tension, balance the emotions, enliven the spirit and stimulate feelings of inner-peace, well-being and hope.
>
> *Jasmine* as its fragrance is uplifting in times of hopelessness and helps reduce anxiety

Neroli, an oil whose fragrance helps release depression and anxiety. It is calming to both body and spirit, restores confidence and brings hope to seemingly hopeless situations.

Orange has a fragrance that is uplifting and helps with depression

For clients wanting to connect more deeply with inner knowing, to their Spirit Guides, or to develop psychic abilities, you may consider diffusing:

Lemongrass, whose fragrance may promote psychic awareness

3 Wise Men creates a sense of spiritual awareness and reverence when diffused

When diffused, the holy oils of *Frankincense* and *Myrrh* promote spiritual awareness, are uplifting and may strengthen meditation.

For a client who has suffered abuse and is unable to release:

Diffusing the blend *Forgiveness* may help activate the desire to forgive and release old, painful emotions

The blend named *Hope* offers a fragrance that creates a feeling of peace and the ability to live life. *Hope* contains the essential oil *Melissa*, which on its own is calming and opens the space for hope.

The blend *Joy* helps stimulate feelings of self-love and confidence. *Joy* is an excellent diffusing choice for those suffering from low self-worth, self-judgment and lack of self-love.

For clients who are fearful for any reason, including a fear of doing inner work because of what they might find or fear of not being able to cope with memories of abuse, the blend *Valor* is an excellent diffusing choice. This fragrance promotes a feeling of protection, strength and courage.

Sacred Mountain is another blend that may be used for fearfulness as its fragrant influence is one of strength, empowerment, grounding and protection.

All of these oils and oil blends are recommended for cold-air diffusing, for preparing your space to receive a client, to assist yourself in your personal meditative process, and/or to generally support you as you go about your day. This list is by no means complete. As you use and experiment with essential oils, you are sure to find more favorites that work well in various situations.

In addition to diffusing oils, **cleaning products** that are environmentally healthy and highly effective include *Thieves Foaming Hand Soap* with its proven anti-bacterial properties. This great-smelling, gentle soap cleanses and purifies the hands while conditioning the skin. *Thieves Household Cleaner* works spectacularly well for cleaning all surfaces. For example, I know of a lovely Buddha fountain that accumulates a green algae. In the past the owner has used bleach to clean it even though she could barely stand the smell and had to wear rubber gloves to protect her hands. She was skeptical that a natural, biodegradable and gentle cleanser would work very well, but was rewarded for her willingness to give it a try and pleasantly surprised by how easy yet thorough it was. Now she can keep her Buddha fountain and other sacred works clean with this good smelling, gentle, high vibrational energy cleaner.

Where to Get Therapeutic Grade Essential Oils

If you are now interested in using therapeutic grade essential oils personally, professionally or both, you will be inspired and pleased with your results. Over many years we have done the research, and whole heartedly recommend *Young Living Essential Oils*.

What makes Young Living Oils different? Do your own research, and start with these questions:

- How many years has the company been working with essentials oils?
- Does the company own and operate its own essential oil research farms? If so, how many farms?
- Is the company proficient in distilling oils?
- Does the company offer a broad enough offering to take care of your health needs?
- Does the company test essential oils to ensure that there are no adulterations? Do they use in-house labs to test each batch? Do they use independent labs to validate their own findings?
- What does the company do in its processes and procedures to guarantee accurate plant identity and oil purity?
- Does the company routinely visit its suppliers to ensure the best manufacturing practices are followed?
- What peer-reviewed research has the company published? Have they tested their oils in clinical settings?
- If the company claims its products are "certified," specifically which essential oil experts have certified it?
- How has the company established its oil standards? How do they know they are selling oils containing the right amounts of constituents to be effective?
- Are the company's oil standards based on their own library of thousands of researched articles, thousands of essential oil gas chromatograph tests, and data from hundreds of thousands of user experiences?
- Does the company have in-house expertise and commitment to quality assurance?

See our website (www.AlchemicalScents.com) for classes, updates AND a wide range of Young Living Essential oils. For Alchemical Scents practitioners, we recommend these oils for starters:

Basic Starter Kit (3 oils)

Young Living Oil	**Resonates with:**
Lavender	Inner Mother
Frankincense	Higher Self
Inner Child	Inner Child

Expanded Basic Kit (5 oils) also includes

Valor	Inner Father
Abundance	Abundance

Free mp3 download: when you purchase the *Abundance* blend from our website, email us: desk@AlchemicalScents.com and we will send you a link to a free download of Linda Baker's guided meditation, ***The Journey Into Abundance*.**

Want help? We are available to assist you in using the oils and would love to learn how *you* share these outstanding products to help others as well as yourself.

If you have questions and comments, please contact us: desk@AlchemicalScents.com

For anyone interested, there is an opportunity to save on the price of these wondrous oils by becoming a Young Living distributor. We can help you. It is a simple process and will introduce you to even more opportunities and abundance. Becoming a distributor allows you to save 24% of the retail cost of all Young Living products and would allow you to pass savings on to your clients, too! See the website to learn more, or send us your questions by email.

References and Resources

Historical and technical information about essential oils was retrieved from the *Young Living Essential Oils* website: *www.youngliving.com*

Peoples Desk Reference for Essential Oils, compiled by Essential Science Publishing, Second Edition (2001) and Third Edition (2004)

Carolyn L. Mein *Releasing Emotional Patterns with Essential Oils* (1998) Vision Ware Press

David Stewart PH.D *The Chemistry of Essential Oils Made Simple* (2005) N A P S A C Reproductions

David Stewart Ph.D. *Healing Oils of the Bible* (2003) Care Publications

Inhibition of Methicillin-Resistant Staphylococcus Aureus (MRSA) by essential oils:
http://thieves-secret.com/pdf/MRSA_article.pdf

Alchemical Hypnotherapy and Somatic Healing
www.alchemyinstitute.com
www.alchemyinstitute.com/somatic.htm

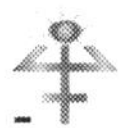

Quick Reference Guide

Issue	Essential Oil
Abundance	Abundance
Acceptance	Acceptance
Anger	Release, Trauma Life
Anti-Bacterial	Lemon, Purification, Thieves
Anti-depressant	Orange, Lemon
Anti-inflammatory	Rose, Orange, Spruce
Antioxidant	Tangerine, Lemon
Antiseptic	Lavender
Anxiety	Lemon
Balance	Spruce, Lavender, Rose
Calming	Cedarwood, Inner Child, Melissa
Change	Awaken
Child	Inner Child
Clarity	Lemon
Cleanse (a room)	Thieves
Cognitive Performance	Lavender
Commitment	Magnify Your Purpose
Confidence	Rose
Connection	Cedarwood
Contentment	Lavender
De-Stress	Rosemary, Lemon
Dizziness	Tangerine
Dreams	Dream Catcher
Emotional Balance	Inner Child
Emotional Blocks	Spearmint, Spruce
Empowerment	Sacred Mountain
Energize	Peppermint
Energy	Lemon
Faith in the future	Envision
Forgiveness, Let Go	Forgiveness, Hope
Future Self	Frankincense, Into The Future
Gratitude	Gratitude
Grounding	Fir, Cypress, Trauma Life
Happy	Rose, Joy

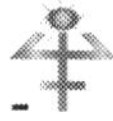

Harmony	Rose, Awaken
Headaches	Lavender
Heart	Joy
Heartburn	Orange
High Blood Pressure	Lavender
High vibration	Rose
Higher Self	Frankincense, Fir, Cedar, Egyptian Gold, 3 Wise Men, Lemon
Hypnosis – Induction	Lavender, Cedarwood, Peace and Calming, Valor
Hypnosis – traumatic memories	Spearmint, Trauma Life
Hypnosis – traumatic release	Release, SARA
Inner Child	Inner Child
Inner Father	Valor, Chivalry
Inner Mate	Jasmine
Inner Mother	Joy, Lavender
Insomnia	Tangerine
Intuitive Abilities	Envision
Leave the Past	Into the Future
Letting Go	Forgiveness
Limbic System	Cedarwood
Memory	Lemon
Menopausal symptoms	Lavender, Orange
Muscle Soreness	Orange
Negative Programming	Sandalwood
Peace	Release, Sacred Mountain
Pick-me-up	Orange
Potential	Awaken
Present Time	Present Time
Procrastination	Acceptance
Prosperity	Spruce, Abundance
Protection	Valor, Sacred Mountain, White Angelica
Relax	Fir, Lavender
Relax	Lavender
Release blocks	Spruce, Forgiveness
Respiratory	Spruce, Cedarwood, Orange
Security	Cyprus, Sacred Mountain
Self-Esteem	Juniper

Self-love	Joy, Ylang-Ylang
Sensuality	Jasmine, Ylang-Ylang
Sleep	Peace & Calming, Lavender, Cedarwood
Somatic Healing	Lavender, Rose, Citrus, Cedar/Spruce and Inner Child
Soothe	Lavender
Spiritually Cleanse (a room)	Cedarwood
Spirituality, Sacred	Frankincense, Fir, Spruce, Galbanum, Myrrh
Strength	Valor
Stress	Vetiver, Lavender
Surrender	Surrender
Trauma	Trauma Life, Vetiver
Uplifting	Peppermint, Myrrh, Melissa, Orange
Visualization	Dream Catcher, Envision
Wellbeing	Balsam Fir

Linda Baker
Master Alchemist
Alchemical Hypnotherapy Practitioner and Trainer

Author of *Soul Contracts - How They Affect Your Life and Your Relationships - Past Life Therapy to Change Your Present Life*; *The Bridge Between Worlds - The Miracle of Following the Heart* and soon to be released *Brain Training*.

Linda graduated as a Registered Nurse and specialized in psychiatric nursing until 1984 when she was introduced to David Quigley and Alchemical Hypnotherapy. Shortly thereafter, Linda left the hospital setting and began to practice with clients as an Alchemical Hypnotherapist. Over the years Linda has studied and incorporated other modalities into her practice with clients: Reiki, OMEGA healing, crystals, sound, essential oils, color, the Reconnection, and most recently, Pranic Healing.

Creative and innovative, Linda continues on her journey of inner transformation while providing the best for clients and the world.

www.alchemicalscents.com
www.innersourceseattle.com

Patricia Haggard
Alchemical Hypnotherapist

Patricia is Co-Director of the Alchemy Institute of Hypnosis in Santa Rosa, CA. When Pat trained in Alchemical Hypnotherapy with David Quigley in 2005, she had many years of prior practice in various complementary care modalities, including Reiki, Reflexology, Astrology, and Sound Therapy as well as a long career in the corporate business world. Currently, Pat and her husband Patrick offer advanced sound, light and mind technologies through their clinic at **Practical Alchemic Therapies** and they also enjoy providing essential business solutions and creative services to small businesses (including hypnotherapists) at **New Leaf Business Pro**.

www.alchemicalscents.com
www.practicalalchemictherapies.com
www.newleafbusinesspro.com

Printed in Great Britain
by Amazon.co.uk, Ltd.,
Marston Gate.